AUTO LEGENDS

Michel Zumbrunn

Text by Robert Cumberford

AUTO LEGENDS

Classics of Style and Design

MERRELL
LONDON · NEW YORK

First published 2004 by Merrell Publishers Limited

Head office
42 Southwark Street
London SE1 1UN

New York office
49 West 24th Street
New York, NY 10010

www.merrellpublishers.com

Publisher Hugh Merrell
Editorial Director Julian Honer
US Director Joan Brookbank
Sales and Marketing Director Emilie Amos
Sales and Marketing Executive Emily Sanders
Managing Editor Anthea Snow
Editor Sam Wythe
Design Manager Nicola Bailey
Production Manager Michelle Draycott
Design and Production Assistant Matt Packer

British Library Cataloguing-in-Publication Data:
Zumbrunn, Michel
Auto legends : classics of style and design
1. Automobiles – Pictorial works 2. Automobiles –
Design and construction – Pictorial works
I. Title II. Cumberford, Robert
629.2'22

ISBN 1 85894 216 0

Produced by Merrell Publishers
Designed by Matt Hervey
Copy-edited by Richard Dawes
Indexed by Alan Thatcher
Printed and bound in China

Jacket front and pages 26–27: Jaguar E-Type, 1961
Jacket back: Citroën 11B 'Traction Avant', 1934
Page 2: BMW 328 Mille Miglia Touring, 1939
Page 5: Bugatti Type 55, 1932

It is my sincere wish to mention and to thank friends and
acquaintances who helped me contact the owners of the
masterpieces in the field of classic cars, and so assisted me in
documenting an important feature of modern design.

Among those many contacts are:
Conte Jacques R. de Wurstemberger, Charles G. Renaud,
Antoine Prunet, Alberto Martinez, Robert Temperli,
Urs P. Ramseier and Lukas Hün

Michel Zumbrunn

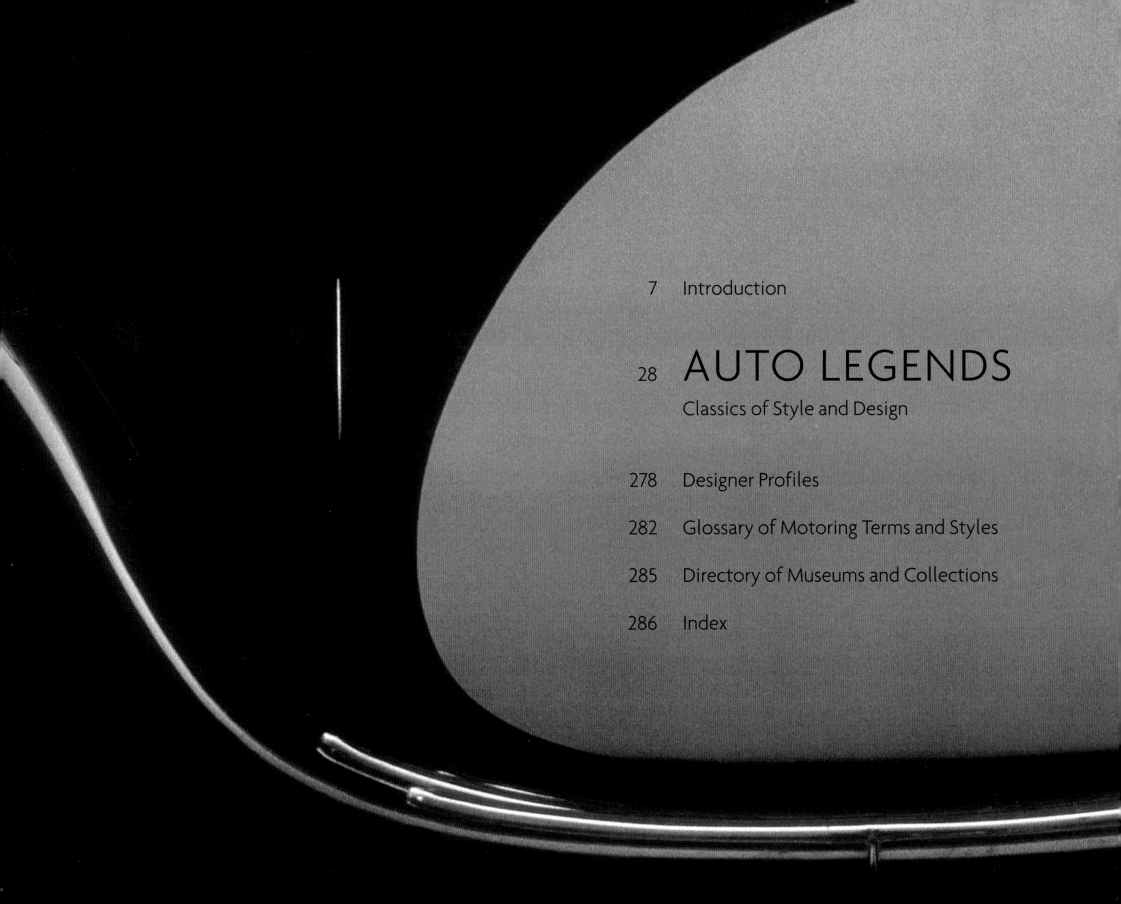

INTRODUCTION

Born in the late nineteenth century as a curious invention that derived from the many advances of the Industrial Revolution, and then taken up by wealthy and daring young men as a sporting device, the car really began to come into its own as an object both utilitarian and aesthetic at the beginning of the twentieth century. In 1914, as Europe was plunged into war on an unprecedented scale, the car was becoming practicable and available to a wider section of society. Until then, the primary thrust of automotive development had been in engineering, in efforts to make cars more reliable and simpler to use. That is not to say that there had been no concern for appearance during the car's developmental period. The carriage builder's art and craft had been refined over hundreds of years, and it was natural that self-propelled carriages should inherit many of the decorative elements of their horse-drawn forebears, however inappropriate they might be for this new means of individual transport.

The car had existed for about twenty-five years as the twentieth century began. By 1940, when its development essentially stopped for five years, it had assumed all of its morphology as we understand it today. Already by 1900 the mechanical architecture of the modern car had been largely established, and many historians consider the 1901 Daimler 'Mercedes' model to have been the finest example. The physical organization of its elements was, from front to back: radiator, engine, gearbox, drivetrain and rear (driving) axle. For the next six decades most cars were constructed in this way, and almost all luxury models built today follow this classical pattern. Mercedes has kept this arrangement for more than a century, apart from a misguided experiment with rear engines in the 1930s, but latecomers to the premium market, such as Toyota with its Mercedes-inspired Lexus saloons, have carefully followed the pattern as well.

above
The first mass-produced car, the 1901 Oldsmobile Curved Dash Runabout really did resemble a horseless carriage.

opposite
The Cord L-29 of 1939 was both technically innovative, with its front-wheel drive, and aesthetically appealing.

FORM AND FUNCTION

The claim that a well-designed and well-built car is a work of art is by no means simply the exaggeration of an over-enthusiastic publicist hoping to sell another few hundred thousands of his employer's mass-produced commodity vehicles. Many cars, although certainly not all, are works of art in the purest sense, representing perhaps the defining physical art of the past hundred years. There is a difference of scale, but not of purpose, between a Fabergé egg made for the Russian court and an exquisitely finished body on a Rolls-Royce chassis bespoken by an Indian maharaja. Both are examples of extraordinary human craftsmanship, objects created to be admired (and envied) down to their least detail.

That the exceptional car also has a mundane function – one of mobility – is almost beside the point. But not entirely so. To have any value, a car must not be just beautiful; it must run, and run reliably. As recently as twenty years ago buyers tolerated operational eccentricities in high-performance cars such as Ferraris and Lamborghinis. No more. Today a man who buys a Porsche expects it to function perfectly, day in, day out, whether it is being used as a shopping trolley or on the racetrack. And, amazingly, Porsches do just that. Maintenance costs are high, but day-to-day reliability is at least as good as, and usually better than, that of mass-produced cars.

In the early days of the car there was thus necessarily a divergence between the ways in which the twin issues of the mechanical elements of a car and human requirements were dealt with. Engineers wanted – and needed – to use the precision and repeatability of machine tools to create engines and drivetrains that were rigorously identical, with interchangeable parts that could be removed and replaced without the ministrations of a highly skilled mechanic. At the same time the bodies that clothed those monuments of precision needed to be quite individual, in order to answer the desire of those economically advantaged persons who could afford cars to be at once individual and in tune with the modes of their era.

In the first half of the twentieth century car bodies evolved from being made up of disparate, discrete elements towards the integration of these into a unified form. In the early days the passenger compartment was totally separate from the 'engine room', and little effort was made to connect the two. In the case of Renault cars, where the radiator stood between the engine cover and the body as a declared element of separation, this was of little importance. But when the radiator was in front, as it was in most cases, the scuttle area made the transition from one solid form to another, its cross-section often changing from round to square in an extremely short distance, rarely with harmonious effect. Luggage was carried outside the car body on racks, from which it would be removed into house or hotel at the end of a trip. We can admire some of those cars today for the craftsmanship that went into building them, but rarely does the whole shape appeal to the senses in the way that more modern sculptural forms do. Early cars can be fascinating, but true beauty of line and form did not come into its own until about 1925.

At the beginning of the twentieth century passengers sat up very high, as they had done in horse-drawn vehicles, with the floor of the passenger compartment above the hub of the wheels. Wheels were typically different in size from front to rear, and very large in diameter. They were constructed with either wooden spokes, like a wagon, or wire tension spokes, like a bicycle. As car shapes evolved, wheels tended to become smaller, and the passengers usually moved forwards and downwards. These tendencies continued throughout the last century, with Chrysler, for example, proclaiming 'cab forward' as a design virtue in the last decade, although all that really happened is that the base of the windscreen was moved forward, to the detriment of visibility and overall proportions. As the twentieth century came to an end, so did that long practice of reducing height, moving passengers forward and fitting ever-smaller wheels. In the closing decade the diameter of wheels went from the almost universal 15 inches (380 mm) back up to 16, 17 and even 22 inches (560 mm). And the increasing popularity of sports utility vehicles (SUVs) and 'people movers' means that seating is once again higher, although not quite at the levels of horse-drawn vehicles.

Illustrations such as this 1930s Delahaye design from Figoni et Falaschi were used to entice prospective clients, who might be offered half a dozen propositions.

CULT OF THE BODY

One is always tempted to compare car bodies to architecture or sculpture. In fact, they are more closely related to clothing. Or, rather, that was the case during the brief but glorious period between 1919 and 1939, before Europe plunged again into a maelstrom, recovery from which totally changed the automotive landscape forever. In those two decades most superior European and American cars were sold as running chassis, with bodywork to be added according to the whim and the means of the buyer. Naturally, most car manufacturers did offer bodies of their own construction, chosen from a catalogue of standard designs, but the possibility always existed of having a car's chassis covered by a body made by a coachbuilder (the horse-drawn terminology stuck) from a different city or even a different country. English bodies were sought for their rigour of construction, Italian for their sense of style and French for their unmistakable elegance.

As with women's fashions, the best-designed car bodies in that benighted inter-war period of unresolved peace came from Paris; not necessarily from Parisian or even French designers, but definitely from Paris. As the centre of the aesthetic automotive universe, that city drew exceptional designers from all over the world. Joseph Figoni from Italy, Howard 'Dutch' Darrin from America, Count Alexis de Sakhnovsky from Russia and hundreds of others moved there. Packards, Duesenbergs, Daimlers, Bentleys, Alfa Romeos, Isotta-Fraschinis – these and dozens of other quality chassis were graced with Parisian bodywork, as were the great French chassis from Hispano-Suiza, Bugatti, Delahaye, Delage and Talbot.

Sir Henry Royce had, quite early on, conceived the idea that bodywork was ephemeral, but that a properly engineered chassis – one of his own, for example – should go on for ever, constantly being dressed in contemporary style. It was a splendid notion, yet mechanical development was so rapid, and fashionable body styles changed so radically, that it was rarely, if ever, implemented. Collectors have found a few cars fitted with their second or third bodies, but it is rare that original purchasers have bothered to keep an early chassis in use with later bodywork.

It is often said that history is written by the victors, and indeed it tends to be a tale of princes, kings and emperors. During the twentieth century the nobility of the automotive world fared no better than royalty in the world at large. Democratization has seen to it that almost every citizen in the developed world enjoys the use of a car – in America today there are more registered cars than licensed drivers. And there is not a single great car maker that is not either wholly owned by a mass manufacturer – Bentley, Bugatti and Lamborghini by Volkswagen, Rolls-Royce by BMW, Alfa Romeo, Ferrari and Maserati by Fiat, Jaguar and Aston Martin by Ford – or totally dependent on one of the giants for the supply of critical components such as engines – as are, for example, Bristol, Lotus, Morgan and a handful of other small firms, most of them British.

This book documents many of the one-off hand-built cars from the early days, but care has also been taken to show us, with precision lighting, the form and details of some of the most common models produced in large volumes. As one follows the development of car design in these pages, one can see that the wheel has turned. Where once ordinary cars were modelled on rare and exalted luxury models, today mass-produced cars set the standard for the vehicles bought by the wealthy and powerful. Such features as are now thought necessary even for the highest-performance exotic cars – air conditioning, automatic transmission, servo-assisted steering, a concert-hall-like sound system – were available on low-cost American Fords, Plymouths and Chevrolets decades before they reached the rarefied level of Europe's finest models.

A key point to note when considering the development of body design is that no one really knew what a car should look like as the twentieth century began. There had been no archetypical car shape in the previous century, at the time when inventors' dreams were becoming commercial realities. Although it was common to think in terms of 'horseless carriages', and many self-propelled vehicles did indeed look much like horse-drawn carriages, with their engines hidden away beneath the seat, inventors and designers were seeking more suitable forms for what was swiftly becoming a widely accepted device, at least in Europe and North America.

INFLUENCES ON BODY DESIGN

During the first two decades of the century many variations were explored, all of them related to other vehicles. The major influences on car design, apart from animal-drawn carriages, were boats and ships, locomotives and – once they came along and everyone could see them – aeroplanes. Later a fifth reference – a self-reference, in fact – was racing cars. Once the bifurcation between touring and racing was well established, and racing cars adopted very narrow bodies while passenger cars got wider and more comfortable, the appeal of slim, low, visually elegant racing-car shapes was transferred to selected passenger models.

Carriages and boats had been developed for millennia, with elegance and ostentation being principal design criteria for upper-class carriages, while elegance and efficiency obtained for boats. It is noteworthy that many early motor vehicles used the overall lines, details and methods of construction developed for carriages. And why not? Carriages had to resist falling apart on bad roads just as early cars did, and the technology, techniques and materials were well known and thoroughly proven. In the early days wood and leather were used more often than the sheet metal we now think of as normal, even essential, for cars.

Boats exerted a different kind of influence. We humans live in the thin envelope of air around our planet much as fish live in water. We don't think of our gaseous atmosphere, and we mostly ignore its viscosity and resistance to our motion. But we have never been able to ignore those characteristics of water when we make boats. Air and water are both fluids, and movement through them requires much the same attention to flow-lines and pressure fields. Seeing and feeling the resistance of water, men tried to resolve the problem of moving through it. Even the most ancient boats known to us were shaped to allow easier penetration of the obstructive fluid, and the most effective hulls were perfected by trial and error. No one looking

The Stanley Torpedo steam-powered racer achieved 195 kph (120.8 mph) in 1906 at Ormond Beach, Florida. The following year it approached 322 kph (200 mph) but crashed.

at the form of such efficient boat hulls can avoid seeing a kind of beauty in them, a beauty related to our perception of the human form, with its gentle curves and elongated limbs.

So it is not surprising that some designers not only used boat forms for inspiration, but applied them to car chassis exactly as they existed for maritime use. The Stanley speed-record steam car that ran in Florida at the turn of the twentieth century really did look like an inverted canoe with external wheels. But a form that may be stable in a highly viscous fluid such as water can be dangerously unstable in a thin fluid such as air, and the driver of the Stanley lost control and crashed at a speed later estimated to be well over 300 kph (186 mph). Nonetheless, boat-like forms continued to be used for cars. If you look at a Bugatti Type 35 from the top, its pointed rear seems much like the prow of a small boat and its flat radiator much like the stern.

To many observers in the nineteenth century, steam locomotives were the icons of the age: huge, heavy iron and steel devices that could move faster on land than any animal could or ever had. No wonder the morphology of the locomotive, with its long boiler in front of a cabin set well back, served as an ideal visual metaphor for car designers. Early carriage-based cars had little huts erected over their engines. Some, France's Renault in particular, made those little huts rather streamlined, inclining rearwards like the inverted prows of boats. Later on, under the influence of locomotives, those little huts became longhouses, impressive forms covering not just the engines, but also the legs of the drivers and passengers; and, in order to maintain the illusion of speed and power, car passenger compartments tended to be as cramped and short as the cabs of locomotives.

There was a good practical reason for this second development: the fireman needed to cross the cab to the coal car behind the locomotive, pick up a shovelful of coal and carry it back across the cab to the firebox. A shorter path was more efficient, so cab lengths were minimized. It took a very long time for car builders to arrive at the proportions of the original Mini, in which 80% of the total length was devoted to the cabin and only 20% to the machinery and luggage. To this day the combination of a long bonnet and a close-coupled passenger compartment appeals to car enthusiasts and the general public alike. There is a sense of potency, of controlled power and potential speed, in long-nosed vehicles.

The influence of aeroplanes on car design was slow to come, in part because they took a long time to develop into what they needed to be in order to fly quickly and well. One of the most beautiful small aeroplanes ever made, the Deperdussin of 1913, embodied most of the characteristics of small racing aeroplanes built decades later, but since it was easier to build trusses (like bridges) than to brace monoplane wings,

Alec Issigonis reserved most of the length of his beloved Mini for passengers and luggage. Only 20% was taken up by the mechanics – a revelation in 1959.

inter-braced biplanes persisted long after they should have been abandoned. Well into the 1940s aeroplanes tended to look like architectural constructs with little relevance to the more dimensionally constrained form of cars. But, as always, there were a few designers who were ahead of the mass, and it happens that one of the most far-sighted aeroplane designers, Marcel Riffard, worked for a car manufacturer, Renault. To see a Caudron-Renault racing aeroplane built over seventy years ago is to see something extremely close to the optimum form possible for a propeller-driven single-engined aeroplane. Yet Riffard's aerodynamic wizardry never had the slightest influence on contemporary Renault cars.

The principal influence of racing cars on passenger-car design came from efforts to create shapes that flowed without break from front to back. This is very much what boat designs did, of course, but the most impressive examples of the influence of aeroplanes are racing sports cars such as the Bugattis that won the Le Mans 24 Hour Race in 1937 and 1939, rather than the passenger cars created with aerodynamics in mind. The commercial failure of the Chrysler Airflow, one of the most significant cars of the 1930s, set back the application of scientific aerodynamic study for cars at least two, perhaps four, decades. Today aerodynamics are of primary importance to designers of passenger cars, but art, science and applied practice have confirmed that what is important for aeroplanes has virtually no relationship to cars.

THE £100 FORD SALOON

The styling of the British Ford Model Y from 1932, designed in America by E.T. 'Bob' Gregorie, was highly influential for years to come.

DEMANDS OF THE MASS MARKET

Once the car became a regular part of daily life in developed countries in the 1920s, commerce was more important than invention. Mass manufacture had begun in 1901 with the little Oldsmobile Curved Dash Runabout (see page 29), but the real trigger for commerce was the development of the moving assembly line set up in 1912 to speed production of the Ford Model T (see page 35), introduced in 1908 and instantly popular because of its simplicity and toughness. Henry Ford sold his cars on the basis of practicality and price (constantly reduced as production efficiencies increased), not style. His rivals – and there were many in America – tried to beat him by making their products more attractive in terms of features and shapes. It is difficult to cite any examples of truly stylish cars from the early 1920s, apart from a few coachbuilt luxury vehicles, but by the beginning of the 1930s style was vital. And when anyone was successful in selling a lot of a particular model, others very quickly made near copies of it.

Thus imitation became a logical way to shape cars. The first car designed for the Ford Motor Company by Eugene 'Bob' Gregorie, its first stylist, was the little British Ford Y, introduced late in 1931 as

a 1932 model. This featured a radiator grille that was pointed at the bottom and leant backwards towards its rectangular top. Edsel Ford, the company's president, liked it so much that he had its theme adapted for the 1933 American Ford models, introduced in 1932. It is in no way surprising that André Citroën, always impressed by American car design and manufacturing methods, should imitate this successful leitmotif for his radical front-wheel-drive cars in 1934. Ford abandoned this particular Gregorie style for 1935, but the Citroën stayed in production in France until 1957.

One of the most imitated car designs ever was the Chrysler (and sub-marque De Soto) Airflow series (see page 100). The engineering basis here was to move the engine forward so that the passenger compartment could be wholly contained within the car's wheelbase. This idea had informed the development of Voisin cars in France even earlier, but Gabriel Voisin, despite having been an aircraft manufacturer, was caught up in the ideas of Cubism and Le Corbusier's architecture. His cars of the 1920s, for all their modern mechanical layout, were agglomerations of block-like forms until the early 1930s, when he finally turned to aerodynamic shapes for his saloons. The Chrysler Airflow was meant to be aerodynamic, like the streamlined diesel-electric locomotives then coming into service in America, but it lacked grace.

The Airflow was a sales disaster, in large part because Walter P. Chrysler insisted on bringing it to market for the tenth anniversary of the company bearing his name, leaving his engineers only fifteen months to develop what was, in fact, a revolutionary design concept. And it did not help that while at first the Airflow concept was intended only for the De Soto, Chrysler decided to make five different wheelbases and three different trim lines. The cars were not ready when they were offered for sale, and people in America were fascinated by, but did not like, the stumpy, rounded-down front ends that were such a contrast with the long-bonnet cars that had preceded the Airflow.

But this aversion was not recognized at first, and engineers everywhere were attracted to the Airflow's mechanical and architectural virtues. In those days, when conventional cars could be designed, tooled and put into production in a year or so (even the radical unit-construction Citroën 'Traction Avant' took only eleven months), the Airflow was widely copied all over the world. Peugeot in France, Toyota in Japan for its first-ever car, Volvo in Sweden, and Fiat in Italy (and by extension Simca in France) all made Airflow-like cars. In 1937 Berliet made cars with Airflow body shapes but more conventional front ends like those Chrysler itself affixed to the Airflow bodies in 1935–37. Imitation might be the sincerest form of flattery, but in this case it was not a brilliant commercial tactic.

above
This hulking Maybach Zeppelin, with bodywork by Spohn of Ravensburg, evolved into a genuinely streamlined design in the mid-1930s.

opposite
Neither the Burlington Zephyr nor the Chrysler Airflow was especially aerodynamic by modern standards, but they captured the public imagination in 1934.

As production volumes rose, new materials were introduced to car manufacture. As late as the mid-1930s mass-produced cars from General Motors, then as now the largest-volume manufacturer in the world, were still using wooden framing for the nominally all-steel 'turret top' bodies of its American marques. Structures made entirely of metal, first employed on Dodge Brothers cars in the 1920s, were much lighter, which in turn permitted closed passenger compartments. By 1925 the majority of cars had enclosed bodies, most of them wood-framed and metal-skinned, although there were intriguing alternatives, including the fabric-skinned Weymann bodies favoured for sporting Bentleys.

THE FULL-WIDTH BODY

The development of bodies that enclosed the wheels completely was slow and sporadic, but persistent and inevitable. One of the earliest full-width bodies without separate covers for the individual wheels was the Hanomag Kommissbrot ('Army bread'), a small, single-cylinder German car made in the 1920. But full bodies were created by Bugatti in 1923 for his unsuccessful 'tank' cars, and by Chenard et Walcker in 1925. Both applications were for racing cars. Full 'pontoon' bodies that prefigured today's cars were offered in the 1930s, although only by specialist manufacturers (the 1933 Pierce Silver Arrow, the 1935 Voisin Aérodyne, and various Spohn aerodynamic bodies on huge Maybach Zeppelin V12 chassis, among others). Morphologically, there is no significant difference between the 1933 Pierce and the 1948 Oldsmobile 98, or between the 1935 Voisin and the 1946 Kaiser (designed by 'Darrin of Paris').

By the end of the 1930s Italian coachbuilders had designed sports-car bodies that in every way described the shape of two-seaters up to the present time. Carrozzeria Touring of Milan developed aerodynamic full-width bodies for BMW that had enormous influence (one of them was effectively the prototype for the 1949 Jaguar XK120). At the end of the 1930s Battista 'Pinin' Farina designed a number of small Lancia racing cars in both open and closed form that still look quite modern to us seventy years later. German body builders, most particularly Spohn, built aerodynamic coupés for racing and touring use. A Spohn Maybach fastback coupé was more than 5.5 metres (18 feet) long, and was intended for high-speed driving on the new autobahns. Front-wheel-drive aerodynamic Adler coupés ran with success at Le Mans in the 1930s as well. But mainstream producers continued right up to the outbreak of World War II in autumn 1939 to make cars with four distinct, individual wing forms, some of them continuing to make an exposed spare wheel a decorative element.

Design evolution is not a "long tranquil river", as poets would have it. There are sudden ruptures, surprising mutations and totally unexpected and unpredictable changes. In car design there have always been a few iconoclastic practitioners who move things forward in radical ways. Gordon Buehrig was one such: his front-wheel-drive 1936 Cord had no radiator grille, an element thought to be so necessary for identity that even the air-cooled Franklin cars, which had no radiators, nevertheless kept a tall grille shape like other cars.

In the late 1930s Bob Gregorie had the idea of turning a radiator through ninety degrees, making it in effect half as high and twice as wide as those of other cars. Gregorie took air into the radiator lower down, in the 'catwalk' between bonnet and wings – a tactic copied almost immediately, first in America, then in Europe. He was also first to put headlights into the wings of popular cars, rather than having them as separate elements, in the 1937 Ford. (The American marque Pierce-Arrow had featured involute conical headlight mounts on the front wings since the 1910s, while the 1936 Lincoln Zephyr had lights in its wings, as designer John Tjaarda had intended from the first in his rear-engined prototype.)

Pinin Farina's 1947 Cisitalia 202 coupé was one of the most influential post-war designs. Its classic purity of form was admired worldwide.

If car manufacture ceased during the early 1940s, car design did not. A great deal of significant work was done unofficially in the back rooms of car companies involved in making war materiel and, when hostilities were over, some of the work done in secret and in designers' spare time was applied. Because the war did not touch America physically, the country was first with pure post-war product. The ancient (in automotive terms, since it had been a carriage maker long before the first car was invented) Studebaker Company had the first truly new car in 1946 for the 1947 model year. Designed by the Raymond Loewy firm, it had an upper body structure that made use of curved glass to create a wrap-around rear window. The body sides were fairly flat and, in order to retain a sense of normality, rear wing shapes were superimposed on the pontoon sides.

This appliqué of a bumper form was paralleled in Italy when Pinin Farina designed the road-going version of the Cisitalia 202 (see page 163). Pinin Farina took the racing coupé designed by Giovanni Savonuzzi, lopped off the exaggerated (but scientifically correct) fins and added vestigial wing shapes at the back. This car, the prototype of which is in the permanent collection of the Museum of Modern Art in New York, was the true herald of the new era in car design.

General Motors was ready with its new designs in the autumn of 1947, when the 1948 Cadillac and Oldsmobile models were introduced. These, too, had rear wing forms applied to pontoon sides, a design scheme applied to all five US General Motors nameplates the following model year (1949). Ford's new cars were ready only for the 1949 model year, and they were decidedly different. The Ford was a flat-sided box

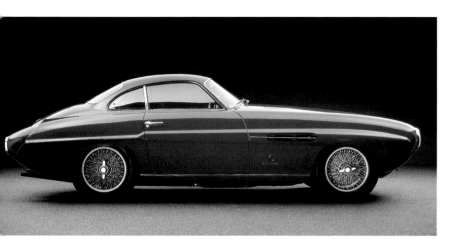

Carrozzeria Ghia applied its 'Supersonic' design to many chassis, but none was more satisfying aesthetically than this 1952 Fiat V8 – a masterpiece.

with horizontal tail lights. Influenced by the lightweight Studebaker, it replaced the fully tooled car that was at first intended to be the post-war Ford. Basically too heavy and too expensive, it was released under the Mercury nameplate.

In Europe, Renault was one of the first manufacturers to come to market with a car completely different from what had gone before. The 4CV saloon, issued in 1948 in only one specification and only one colour, had its engine in the rear, driving a three-speed gearbox tucked under the rear seats. The styling was unremarkable, but at least it was original, whereas the rear-engined Volkswagen that had been resurrected by the British occupants of the northern sector of western Germany was, as far as its shape was concerned, a pre-war copy of the De Soto Airflow. In France, Citroën continued with the 1934 11CV, Renault kept making the Juvaquatre it had copied from Opel, and Peugeot continued the 402 Chrysler Airflow copy.

Most late-1940s cars in Britain and Europe were simply reissues of 1930s models, very little changed in appearance or specification. The destroyed nations were glad to have cars of any kind, and there was no rush to the new. Nor, despite their clearly new bodies, were most of the American cars technically advanced; they simply carried over pre-war engines and chassis. And politics was dictating the future of European car design. In both France and Italy, Communist-dominated labour unions possessed great political power. How that power was used determined what would happen in car design. French Communists – powerful in government as well as in unions – were hostile towards the rich and those whose businesses catered to them.

This, of course, meant the manufacturers of luxury-car chassis and the *carrossiers* who clothed these chassis. Manufacturers such as Delage, Delahaye and Talbot were systematically deprived of raw materials, as were the body builders. Confiscatory taxation on engines of more than 2.8 litres, first established to keep the Ford Model T (2.9 litres) from harming local industry, were strengthened, so few could afford, either financially or in terms of being ostracized, to order a French luxury car. A few cars were made, but the struggle to remain afloat did little to liberate creativity, and French coachbuilt cars, like mass-produced models, tended to resemble what had gone before.

ITALIAN ASCENDANCY

Italy has always been the land of the *combinazione*, a way of working things out so that everyone concerned is satisfied, even the long-suffering tax man. Italian Communists were more concerned with keeping the maximum number of people working than worrying about whether what they were working on might benefit a rich person. Indeed, everyone thought it a fine idea to build expensive, luxurious cars to export, even if that meant diverting scarce metals to small-volume car builders and *carrozzieri*. These provided plenty of jobs. And so was launched the Italian hegemony in car design, led by Pinin Farina's Cisitalia coupé but followed on by lovely bodies created by Allemano, Bertone, Boano, Stabilimenti Farina, Frua, Ghia, Touring, Vignale and hundreds of other, smaller shops that built cars one at a time, usually on Fiat chassis. Fiat, virtually alone in the post-war period, built coachbuilder's platforms, even for its unit-construction cars. Lancia and Alfa Romeo were more reluctant to sell chassis to Luigi or Gianni with their modest workshops, but they did work with the big names.

Modena, home of Ferrari, has a staunchly Communist local government to this day, yet it was the nexus for exotic car production by Ferrari and Maserati, Lamborghini and Pagani, De Tomaso and Bugatti (revived by an Italian dreamer who bought rights to the hallowed name) and many another small firm. Stanguellini, Moretti and at least a hundred other manufacturers who made half a dozen or so cars before disappearing were a fertile source of ideas in both engineering and design. Indeed Enzo Ferrari, once a semi-successful racing driver, then a very successful racing team manager for Alfa Romeo, decided to set up his own racing and sports car firm in the Modena suburb of Maranello. Inspired by Packard Twin Sixes he had seen during World War I, he chose to make a 1500 cc V12 as his first model, and the firm has continued to champion that engine type for more than fifty years.

Ferrari's venture, Germany's Porsche and Japan's Honda are the only car makers, of the hundreds launched after 1945, to have survived and prospered in business. That is, they are the only independent firms left that are making more than 2500 cars each year. At any given moment there are usually a dozen or so brave small-scale companies striving in England, and fewer than that in other countries, and others, such as Saab, that are no longer independent entities. And of course it is too early to predict the longevity of recently created Korean, Chinese and Malaysian car makers.

Great designers abounded in northern Italy, and Turin in the 1950s and 1960s became what Paris had been in the 1920s and 1930s. Just as France had attracted talent from all over the world, so northern Italy enticed people to come and make exciting, beautiful cars. Tom Tjaarda, American son of a brilliantly successful car designer, was one. Alessandro De Tomaso from Argentina was another. His compatriot Horacio Pagani is active today, and many other nationalities are represented among the active designers in the area. Even now designers go to Italy to participate in the creative ferment, although the small, one-off coachbuilders are no

This beautiful object is, in fact, a tool: a pure racing car meant for open-road competition. The sport was still taking place in Italy in 1954 when Pinin Farina created this Ferrari 375 Mille Miglia.

more and what remains are design houses that do more engineering than styling. Ferrari's first in-house designer, the polyglot Frank Stephenson, has an American passport, but he speaks half a dozen languages and has lived for years at a time in Turkey, Tunisia, Spain, Germany and the USA. Ken Okuyama, born in Japan, is now creative director at Pininfarina, where he previously designed several key concept cars before taking time out to teach at California's Art Center College of Design in Los Angeles.

THE TEACHING OF CAR DESIGN

In 1950 the Art Center was virtually the only school in the world that recognized car design as a unique discipline. Many of the best designers in other countries came from engineering backgrounds, or were simply artistically inclined individuals, as was Giorgietto Giugiaro, the best-known and probably most successful independent designer working today. In the past thirty years or so educational courses in car design have been developed in countries all over the world. A car-design contest for schools first organized by the Canadian International Auto Show in Toronto four years ago brings entries from schools in China and India, as well as the usual countries with established car-making operations – nineteen of them at last count. Among the leading schools today are the Royal College of Art in London, Britain's Coventry University, Pforzheim University in Germany, the Center for Creative Studies in Detroit and the Istituto Europeo di Design in Turin.

Today there are so many excellent art, design and engineering schools with courses in car design that there are many more highly talented, well-trained and keen car designers than there are places in design companies. This means that there are enthusiastic, even passionate, designers who will never find a direct means of expression in car design. However, because the car represents one of the most complex and difficult design tasks, anyone capable of solving the problems inherent in its design is well placed to use his or her talent and skill in other aspects of industrial product design.

In perhaps no other profession do we find such internationalism as exists in car design. For many years Italian-born Bruno Sacco directed design at Mercedes-Benz; American Chris Bangle was leader at BMW; British designer Peter Horbury led Volvo design; and another Briton, Trevor Creed, runs Chrysler design. Danish-born Henrik Fisker runs Ford's North American advanced design studios in California and retains the design directorship for Aston Martin. In 2004 Dutchman Adrian van Hooydonk has been named to run BMW brand design as Bangle moves up to overall design direction of BMW Group, which includes the two British marques Rolls-Royce and Mini, and Horbury takes over Ford's North American design for

Ford, Mercury and Lincoln cars and trucks. An Italian, Walter de' Silva, runs the Audi design studios and a Belgian, Dirk van Braeckel, leads Bentley design.

Although Asian companies prefer to keep the top job title for their own countrymen, gifted multi-national designers have nonetheless created many cars from Korea, Japan, Taiwan and China. And English is the lingua franca of the car business (in the French–Japanese merger of Renault and Nissan it is used for all meetings and all official documents), so it is not surprising that so many British designers are present in the world's design studios. Britain essentially no longer has its own car industry, its business leaders having proved themselves as inept as its designers were outstanding – a situation that has caused most British car makers to fall into the hands of American and German companies.

Among other things, the leaders of Britain's car industry decided to outsource much of its design work to Italy. Bristol and Aston Martin turned to Carrozzeria Touring for some of the most cherished models bearing their nameplates. Jensen enlisted the aid of Vignale, and the British Motor Corporation in its Austin-Morris fusion days relied on Pininfarina, as did Donald Healey for his Nash-Healey roadsters. Giovanni Michelotti drew up a number of designs for Triumph, and even Jaguar, proudest champion of in-house design (although it had eagerly copied a Touring BMW to derive its XK120 roadster in 1949), had Pininfarina spruce up its XJ6 and XJ12 saloons for the Series Three models. Zagato was called on to develop a lightweight racing coupé for Aston Martin, and the American importer 'Wacky' Arnolt had Bertone build a series of coupés on MG-TD chassis and some remarkable aerodynamic roadsters for Bristol chassis.

If the venerable AC Cars Ltd did not deal directly with an Italian design house, it did license a design from special builder John Tojeiro that had a body design copied (without credit or royalties) from the *barchetta* ('little boat') roadsters that Touring created for Ferrari in 1947–48. The resulting AC Ace was first powered by the firm's own light-alloy OHC six, a version of a Zeppelin dirigible engine copied in scaled-down form in 1921. This chassis was subsequently fitted with Bristol and Ford six-cylinder engines, and finally was used to make the original Shelby Cobra with American Ford V8 power. Touring also did without credit for the Jaguar XK-D racing sports cars that cribbed the elliptical cross-section of Alfa Romeo's Disco Volante concept cars. This same section was used for the indigenous E-Type, a magnificent all-British design.

Britain was not alone in using Italian designers and design houses. Early Mazda cars were done by Bertone, and Italian design influence was persistent in Japan and, later, in Korea. Giugiaro's ItalDesign shaped the first Korean car, the Hyundai, and many Daewoo models were Giugiaro's as well. Toyota used

The 1953 AC Ace is derived from the Special by John Tojeiro, which in turn was a copy of a Ferrari. It evolved into the Cobra, a car that is still being made.

The simple, straightforward, but brilliant design by Giorgietto Giugiaro made the 1975 Volkswagen Golf the model for tens of millions of family cars.

Giugiaro's Jaguar Kensington concept for its Lexus saloons – those not copied directly from Mercedes S-class models – and it is well known that Pininfarina has collaborated over a long period with Honda, although without direct attribution.

In France, Peugeot began a long relationship with Pininfarina in the early 1950s with the 403 model, a relationship that continued for decades until Pininfarina sold the same design to too many clients at the same time and strained the entente between the companies. The Peugeot 205, the design that saved Peugeot from financial disaster, was done in-house, not by the Italian company, and Peugeot's own designers have designed most current Peugeots. Citroën copied Pininfarina's BMC concept cars to come up with the shapes of its GS and CX saloons, and subsequently relied on Bertone for its Xantia and XM models. Even state-owned Renault relied on Marcello Gandini for its Super Cinq, although the original Renault 5 was the work of its own Michel Boué and design leader Gaston Juchet. Giugiaro designed the Renault 21 body as well as producing designs for American Motors, then owned by Renault.

Elsewhere in Europe, Bertone designed and built coupé models for Volvo, Michelotti designed a coupé for BMW, Frua designed several models of Glas cars – a few of which carried BMW badges after the Munich company bought the assets of Hans Glas – and the most successful Volkswagen of all time, the Golf, was a pure original concept from ItalDesign Giugiaro. Now in its fifth iteration and designed internally, the Golf owes its characteristic shape to the Italian maestro. So did the Simca and Plymouth Horizon models, so closely copied from the VW that the French designers who worked on the project called it the 'Flog' – 'Golf' spelled backwards.

THE US–ITALIAN CONNECTION

In the early 1950s America still had several independent car companies, including Crosley, Nash, Packard, Hudson, Kaiser-Frazer, Willys and Studebaker, along with a dozen nameplates from the 'Big Three' companies: Chrysler, Ford and General Motors. If General Motors tended to set styling trends, having already proposed the wrap-around windscreen seen on the Le Sabre and Buick XP-300 concept cars in 1951 and started the tail-fin craze in 1947 with Franklin Hershey's 1948 Cadillac, there were Italian influences at Chrysler, which used Carrozzeria Ghia in Turin to build a series of concepts and show cars.

Hudson, which had introduced a radical 'step down' design for 1948, used Carrozzeria Touring to build a few prototypes of the car it hoped to manufacture, but the company's directors had chosen to invest what little capital it had available in a disastrously ugly small car rather than in a V8 engine. Staying with side-valve sixes was industrial suicide, and Hudson was merged with Nash Kelvinator, which itself had been aligned with Pininfarina, who had created a line of inelegant, bloated boxes for it. How much of the car was really designed by the Italian firm and how much by in-house designers remains unclear, but given the traditional classicism and formal perfection of Pininfarina's work, it seems likely that a good initial concept was spoiled in the process of production engineering.

Even GM turned to Pininfarina in the 1950s and 1960s to assemble a series of Cadillac models, and then did the same thing in the 1980s with a complicated programme that involved flying Boeing 747s filled with chassis parts without powertrains from Detroit to Italy and roadster bodies from Turin to Detroit. This ill-fated and costly project stopped just as the Cadillac Allante finally became technically competent, but it highlighted the transition the key Italian design houses had been making throughout the 1970s and 1980s, as legislation worldwide made it all but impossible to build one-of-a-kind cars.

Fiat, long dominant in Italy, finally absorbed all of the Italian car industry – first Lancia, then Alfa Romeo, wresting it away from Ford. Fiat had worked with and subsidized Ferrari for years, and then bought Maserati from De Tomaso, tucking it into Ferrari. For whatever reason, Fiat ceased to make the coachbuilder's platforms for its mainstream cars, which within a few years caused hundreds of small body shops to close. Only those design houses with extensive engineering capability, such as ItalDesign, that could offer turnkey factory projects to Third World clients, or those with some production capacity, such as Pininfarina and Bertone, remained as viable business entities.

Even those companies have been in precarious financial circumstances at times, especially when contracts – such as Pininfarina's for the Cadillac Allante or for the production of Peugeot convertibles, or Bertone's to assemble a closed motorcycle for BMW – were cancelled. By the end of the twentieth century Italy had lost its design leadership while retaining the capability to make prototypes more quickly and at lower cost than any other country. Even that capability is under challenge, with a recent Aston Martin prototype having been built in India, and Moroccan and Russian builders showing prototypes in Western European motor shows to solicit business. Cars as beautifully finished as the Cadillac V16 from the 2003 Detroit Motor Show were made in their home countries.

Still, it is hard to imagine that the long Italian metalworking tradition, harking back to the time when suits of armour were lovingly crafted in northern Italy, or the Italian tradition of beautiful buildings and

objects, should wither away. One of the elements that have sustained the Italian hegemony in car design is the constant production of such extraordinary vehicles as the many Ferrari road cars offered over the past forty-eight years, the exceptional Lamborghini cars, the occasional exceptional Alfa Romeo. These beautiful objects make the whole world dream and add to the lustre of Italian design. But remember that French cars and bodies had the same role sixty-five years ago. Nothing is immutable.

AMERICAN INFLUENCE

For many years America's huge car industry, and the gigantic market the USA represents, had tremendous influence on world car design. If you look at a 1957 Mercedes 180 saloon from above, you immediately recognize that, apart from the traditional grille, the car is a copy of 1950–51 Plymouth bodywork. Or look at the 1960 Mercedes with its twisted tail-fin rear wing, almost a carbon copy of the 1957 Rambler. The Volvo 122 Amazon was often thought to have been built off tooling for the Aero Willys of 1953–54, although it was simply 'inspired' by the Phil Wright design, minus its vestigial fins. Volvo built a 'Philip' prototype in the 1950s that was almost a clone of the last Kaiser, a Howard 'Dutch' Darrin design with a heart-shaped windscreen. The brilliantly innovative Citroën DS19 of 1955 was nothing more than a superimposition of the lines of Raymond Loewy's 1953 Studebaker Starliner coupé over the mechanical layout of the 1934 Traction Avant, itself a copy of an American design.

I have discussed the seminal Chrysler Airflow, but an even more influential American design – and an even worse failure in the marketplace – was the 1960 Chevrolet Corvair. Created by Ned Nickles and Budd Sugano, with a front-end theme by Irv Rybicki, during the reign of William Mitchell (Harley Earl's successor as the head of GM Styling), its shape resonated with the world design community.

The Corvair was a pale copy of the early 1930s Hans Ledwinka mechanical layout, as appropriated by Porsche for the KdF Volkswagen, so far as the rear engine and swing-axle suspension were concerned, and it was notoriously unstable and hard to control with its typical American ultra-slow steering. But the styling was so brilliant that copies followed for years. BMW, with the 1600, NSU with its Prinz, Hino with the Contessa, Hillman with the Imp, Panhard with the CT 24, Fiat with the 1500, Zaporozhets in the Soviet Union, even to some extent Renault with the R-8, and of course many of GM's own cars, in particular the 1961 Oldsmobile, all followed the Corvair's lead. There was a perimeter line below the belt that swung completely around the car, with a concave section beneath it. The BMW did not dip in front between the headlights, but in most of the other cars even that characteristic was copied.

And there can be no doubt that the wrap-around windscreen imposed by Harley Earl from the early 1950s and generalized on every GM car by 1955 was influential. Even Pinin Farina used the GM windscreen shape on Lancia Aurelia roadsters, where it was an incongruous addendum. Perhaps the most absurd application of what was, finally, a poor idea both functionally and structurally was on the German DKW Sonderklasse, in which the dogleg windscreen base disfigured a typical middle-European body shape of the late 1930s.

There are other pieces of evidence for American influence. Some, such as mid-1950s Vauxhall and Opel cars, were to be expected, since those makes were owned by GM and their designs, if not executed by GM Styling, were ordered and approved by Harley Earl. But examine the last Borgward cars of 1959 and you will see clear signs of American inspiration. And most Toyota and Datsun (Nissan) models were simply scaled-down American car shapes, many of them ludicrous. The early Toyota Celica coupés had most of their rear-end details copied directly from the first Mustangs, and there are innumerable other cases where American styling, in both its excesses and its successes, was central to world car production.

As this book goes to press a new generation of chief stylists is moving into place, men (and women, at last) in their late thirties to early fifties, experienced in design and part of a cohort that does not necessarily know from direct experience how cars work mechanically, nor how they are put together. In one sense these people are pure stylists, since their knowledge of engineering is not particularly germane to the work they do. What matters today, when all cars are far more reliable, capable, safe and satisfying than the best cars were four or five decades ago, is that they should be attractive and desirable, able to inspire the public to buy them. Ultimately the task of every person in the car industry is to sell cars. Today's designers are actually far better qualified to perform that task than their forebears were.

The rear of the 1971 Toyota Celica – a Japanese copy – is almost a clone of the 1965 Ford Mustang, with more quality and less performance.

NOTE ON THE TEXT

The dates used in this book are based on *The Beaulieu Encyclopedia of the Automobile*, ed. N. Georgano, 2 vols., London (Stationery Office) 2000. Those given in the headings represent the year in which each car was officially launched, with the exception of US cars, which use an autumn model year designation. The illustrations may show models of a later date.

AUTO LEGENDS

1901 OLDSMOBILE CURVED DASH RUNABOUT

A 'horseless carriage' in the concept's purest and simplest expression, the little two-seater imagined by Ransom Eli Olds is historically significant in that it was the first mass-produced car. More than 10,000 units of the simple single-cylinder device were turned out by methods that owed something to the American firearms industry, where the use of interchangeable parts began, but which were certainly more primitive than Henry Ford's later moving production line.

This little car's success was accidental. Olds had prepared a number of larger vehicles, but before production of any of them could begin a fire ravaged the company's premises, and only the little Runabout was saved. Investors wanted to see the beginning of a return on their money, so it was decided to proceed with just the smallest vehicle that had been planned. It is quite possible that so many Runabouts were bought because they looked very like the vehicles the public were used to seeing on the streets. But the Oldsmobile was soundly engineered, reliable by the standards of the day, and it was easy to drive. Oldsmobile was the oldest American marque still operating when General Motors, which had acquired the company in the 1920s, announced in 2000 that it would be closed down.

Oldsmobile was known for advanced engineering, its 1949 model being given one of the Kettering overhead-valve V8 engines. An Oldsmobile Rocket 88 won Mexico's 3500-km (2180-mile) Carrera Panamericana, the world's longest open-road race, in 1950. In the 1980s it was the third-best-selling marque in America.

In 1904 Olds himself started another car company, Reo, its name derived from the initials of his name. Quite handsome cars were made until the mid-1930s, after which the company made only trucks until its demise after World War II.

It is easy to imagine a horse standing in front of this vehicle, and that may well have increased its acceptance at the turn of the last century, when cars were little known in America. There was nothing new or frightening about its appearance.

1907 ROLLS-ROYCE LONDON–EDINBURGH SILVER GHOST

If the architecture of the London–Edinburgh Silver Ghost was essentially that of the first 'modern' car, the 1901 Mercedes (front to back: radiator, engine, gearbox, drivetrain, rear axle), its lithe elegance owes nothing to German practice. The base of the windscreen essentially bisects the wheelbase, giving as much importance – and as much room – to the mechanical section of the car as to the passengers.

What sets this particular sporting model apart from earlier cars, including the first of the Silver Ghost series, is the fact that the bodywork is of equal height above the chassis rails all the way from the outer edge of the radiator shell to the back of the body side, or from front wheel centre to rear wheel centre. The wings cannot accurately be described as 'mudguards': since they are not sealed to the body, they allow a great deal of surface detritus, whether mud, water or dust, to bedevil the passengers. However, they are excellent at limiting aerodynamic drag, thereby considerably increasing the car's potential top speed. Aerodynamic awareness is also shown in the fact that the upper portion of the windscreen is inclined rearwards, rather than sitting vertically as in most cars of this period.

One can infer the extraordinary quality of Sir Henry Royce's engineering from the number of Silver Ghosts still in use today; not everyday use, obviously, but in sporting trials for old cars, including transcontinental runs in North America on public highways with cars ninety years younger. The chassis frame is well above the wheel centres and runs the length of the car with no bends or kick-ups – very much a continuation of horse-drawn vehicle practice in the placement of axles and springs.

above
The Spirit of Ecstasy has graced Rolls-Royce cars for a century. Today it is hard to imagine that there was any whiff of scandal surrounding the sculptor's model.

opposite
One rarely sees cars like this, with the folding top erected. In this case there is a certain raffish elegance, with the line of the tension straps crossing the wing to form an arrow point, and the canvas resembling a flat cap.

There is no mistaking the sporting
purpose of this spare design.
The simple body surfaces are
handsomely framed by the curved
wings and beautifully decorated by
the disparate functional elements.

From the rear, the Silver Ghost
more clearly shows its age, with its
timeless radiator hidden from view
and the long bonnet foreshortened.

1908 FORD MODEL T TOURING

Perhaps the most important car of all time, the Ford Model T was both an engineering and a social milestone. Introduced to an indifferent market in 1908, it had two major virtues from the beginning: it was easy to drive, with its semi-automatic planetary gearbox, and it was tough as old boots, thanks to the use of the highest-quality steel available at the time. With the suspension mounted to the chassis only at the centreline of the car, no amount of twisting and racking over unmade roads would break a Ford, and it was so simple in conception that virtually any farmer could repair it. As sales volumes rose, Henry Ford reduced his prices, thereby increasing sales and permitting still lower prices. By 1925 the T roadster cost just $260.

Ford was first to use a moving assembly line for car manufacture, first to propose a five-day work week, the first industrialist to offer substantial wages – $5 a day was a princely sum that permitted Ford employees to buy Ford cars – and one of the first to use time-and-motion studies in the search for efficient production. The famous dictum "any colour you want, so long as it's black" came from the simple fact that black paint dried faster than any other in the days before spray painting, allowing production to reach 9000 units a day by 1925. The blue paint on the early car seen here was one of several standard choices until Ford's discovery put an end to diversity.

By keeping the T in production too long, Ford lost his tremendous lead over all competitors, but the car put the world on wheels, made America the leader in car manufacturing and changed the way people thought about cars. There is no unifying design theme for the body. Even the last T, in 1927, was just an agglomeration of disparate shapes.

There is obviously no attempt at formal composition in the different elements of this four-seat touring car, yet there is a certain elegance in its various polished metal parts. This is an early version of the 'Tin Lizzie', one of the most beloved and most widely distributed cars of all time.

1914　PIC-PIC TOURER

There is nothing really special about the Swiss Pic-Pic other than its amusing cuckoo-clock name (derived from Piccard-Pictet), but it is an excellent example of what took place in the early days, when enthusiasm for the idea of cars ran high. When manual labour costs were low, there were fine mechanical engineers in every country just waiting to have a crack at making a car, and credulous investors, each dreaming of being the next Ford, thrust money at anyone with a plausible scheme. The problem was not in making a car or two, but in discovering how to make a lot of them and – above all – how to sell them.

This is a stately vehicle, but one without much to recommend it aesthetically. We can imagine that Swiss precision was employed throughout its manufacture – a conjecture supported by the fact that this car is in fine fettle today and works as well as it did when new – but it is without distinction, just like hundreds of other contemporary makes. The dual windscreens are nice, but V-shaped screens were common on boats and frequently seen on other cars. The wings are exceedingly ordinary, without the elegant flow or the curves that would soon arrive on other cars. There is an unnecessary kink in the scuttle (cowl) between the back of the bonnet and the top sill of the bodywork, and no effort was made to integrate the many lights, horns, emblems and mascots into a cohesive whole.

As a monument to the past it is splendid, and few enthusiasts would not be pleased to own such a fine example of early automobilia, but in the great flow of automotive history it simply stands as a surrogate to hundreds of other almost-but-not-quite makes. As such it is worthy of our attention.

above
Avian motifs were common on early cars, but there is little in the car itself to suggest the lightness of flight.

opposite
The tortured sheet metal surfaces of today's BMW cars are nothing compared to the way in which the Pic-Pic's contorted bonnet changes between the concave leading edge and the convex scuttle panel. The windscreens are the best visual elements of the car.

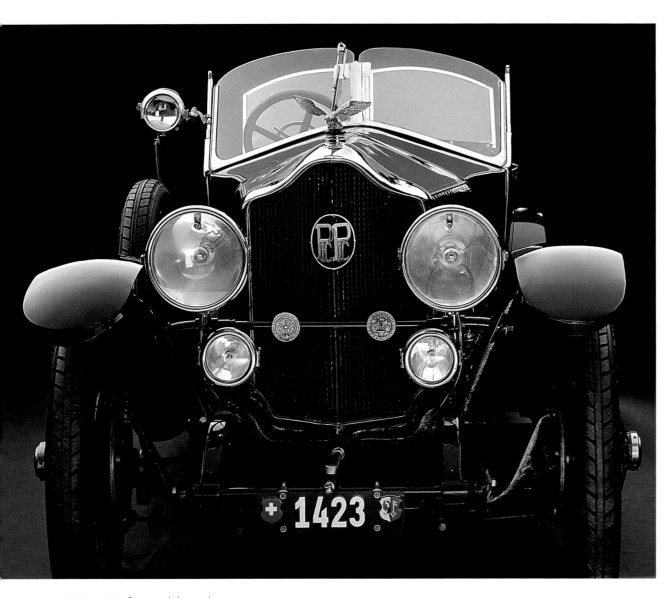

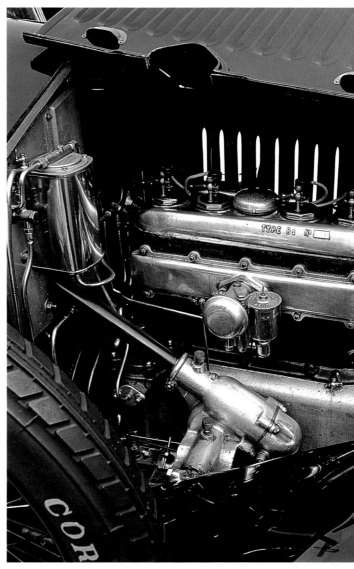

An imposing front end shows the precision metalworking skills of Swiss craftsmen to advantage, but the composition is disjointed and complicated.

The most elegant part of the engine compartment is the beautifully shaped steering box in the foreground. The engine itself is clean but ordinary.

opposite
The unframed glass in the V-shaped screen is elegant, but by modern standards extremely dangerous. The operating controls are all substantial and generously proportioned.

1915 PACKARD TWIN SIX

Early in the twentieth century quality cars were greatly differentiated from popular models in terms of size, performance and finish, but not particularly in terms of style. The old rich in every society tend to be extremely conservative, so those who adopted the new and slightly suspect motor carriage preferred their vehicles to be not too distant from their horse-drawn carriages. Racy lines were definitely not wanted, whereas rigorous vertical windscreens and radiators and rectilinear massiveness were prized. What the gentry accepted, other classes desired. So middle-class respectability suggested that popular cars, to the extent that there were any, ought to look like the cars the rich possessed: sober and upright vehicles.

Discriminating rich Americans chose Packard cars not only for their restrained appearance, but also for their exceptional smoothness of operation. Packard engineers reasoned that if six-cylinder engines were harmonically smooth, twice that many cylinders would be better still. There had been a few experiments with V12 engines earlier, but in 1915 Packard was first to produce and sell what it chose to call the 'Twin Six'.

The model featured here, built in 1916, exemplifies the solidity and seriousness of Packards without being a particularly beautiful object, although Packards evolved into some of the most beautiful cars of the 1930s while retaining their conservative elegance. Enzo Ferrari claimed that he made V12s for the first cars to carry his own name because he had been so impressed by Packard Twin Sixes brought to Europe by Americans during World War I. He was not alone: the Twin Six inspired numerous other manufacturers to make V12s, most of them in the early 1930s at a time when the economic depression virtually guaranteed that they would all disappear. Taking into account aircraft and marine engines, it is likely that Packard made more twelve-cylinder engines than any other firm, before or since.

Staid, even stolid, the Twin Six leaves no doubt that it is a substantial vehicle. The thoroughness of the engineering can be seen in the wooden wheels: lighter and simpler in front, where no braking forces apply, but with more spokes at the rear to accept driving and braking torques.

1919 FARMAN A6B SUPER SPORT

Henry Farman was quite a personality: intrepid pioneer aviator, the first to make a circular flight of more than a mile in public, in a Voisin aeroplane; early aeronautical entrepreneur (with his brothers Dick and Maurice); airline operator; and, after World War I, car manufacturer. The Farman A6B chassis, laid out in 1919 using the Farman brothers' aeronautical engineering background, was an extremely high-quality design, but it was also extremely expensive, even by the standards of Hispano-Suiza or Bugatti. Despite having an aluminium engine (derived from the Farmans' experience with aeroplane engines) and extensive use of aluminium in the bodywork – this example, made for the Maharaja of Idar, is finished entirely in unpainted brushed-alloy sheet – the cars were quite heavy, weighing in at some two and a half tonnes. The company claimed that "an automobile rolls, a Farman glides", but only 120 A6Bs were made between 1919 and 1930, and the company abandoned car making in 1932.

The lines of this A6B are graceful and rather advanced for 1919. There is no hiding the fact that the car is tall and looks heavy, but the flowing lines of the wings and the straight waistline are to its advantage, giving it the appearance of a car made ten years later. The boat-tail shape is unusual on a car with four seats; usually boat-tail speedsters were two-seaters.

The lavish use of aluminium in this model's construction may account for the fact that only 4 cars out of the 120 made are known to have survived. Cars with extensive aluminium content were much prized as scrap during World War II and so were often broken up and melted down for war materiel.

above
For once, the flight motifs are appropriate. The Farman brothers were indeed pioneer aviators, and both the mascot and badge were well earned.

opposite
An unusual aspect of the Farman front end is the absence of a transverse bar on which the headlights could be mounted. The individual pedestals are elegant in advance of their time.

left
Beautifully organized and
beautifully presented, the Farman
engine compartment would please
any constructor.

opposite
With its faired wheels and its
radiused bonnet, which flows
into the body side in a continuous
line, this car might have seemed
advanced ten years after it was
manufactured.

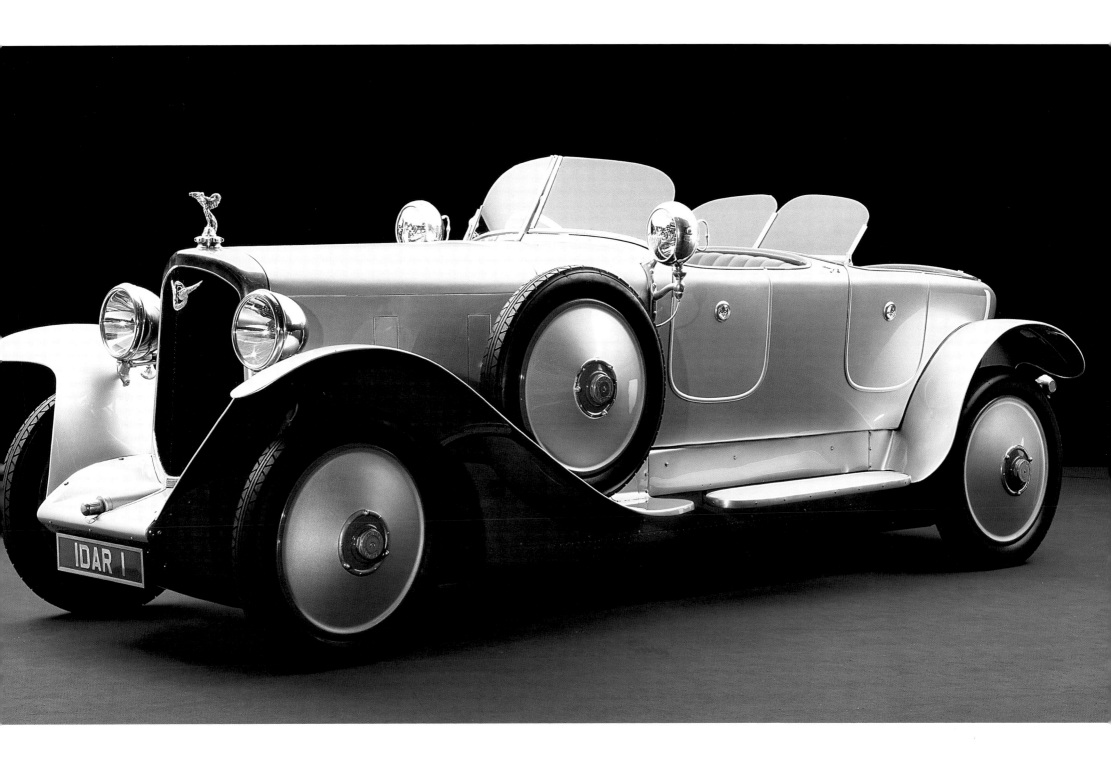

above

Even a simple part of the bodywork, such as this wheel centre, reveals a tremendous amount of intricate machine work and careful hand-fitting – which explains the high price.

left

Whimsical rear lamps show the enormous amount of careful handiwork that went into making this magnificent machine.

opposite

If confirmation of aeronautical inspiration for the Farman design were needed, the disastrous ergonomics of the shotgun-placed instrumentation, as careless as in almost all early aeroplanes, is the final proof. The tight curve at the cockpit edge is prescient, and quite beautiful with it.

The transition of the soft radius along the bonnet and the body side into a hard line towards the boat-tail is astonishingly modern, as are the horizontal decorative elements across the lower portion of the tail.

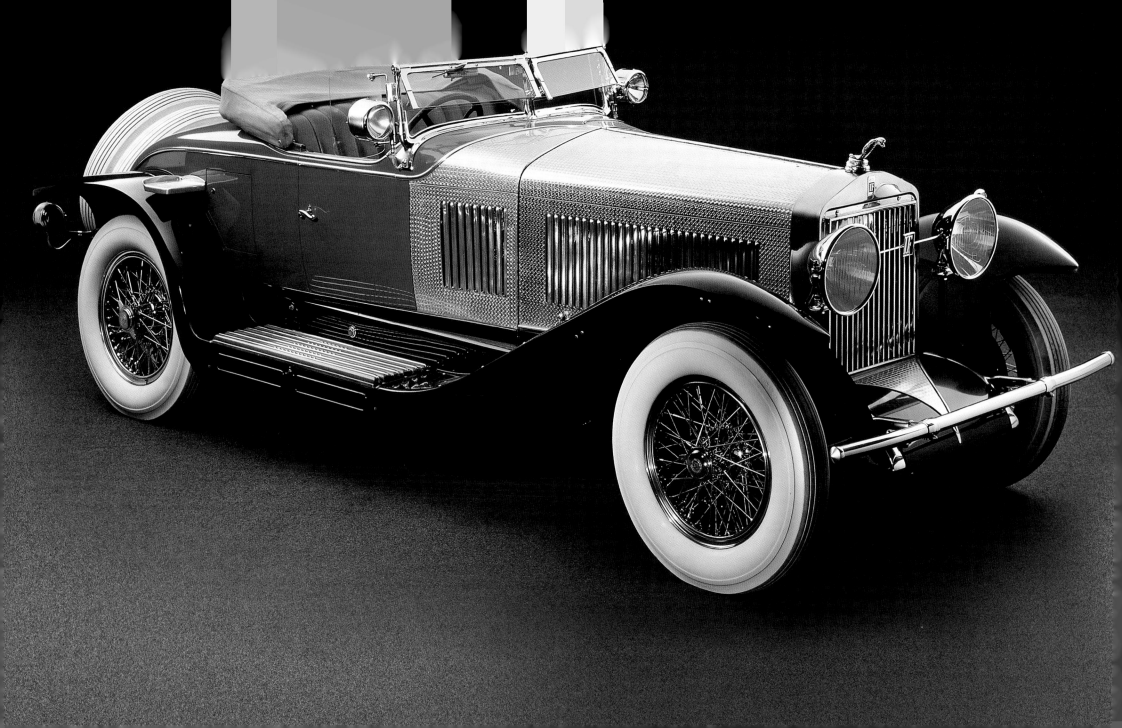

1919 ISOTTA-FRASCHINI 8A FLEETWOOD

The Isotta-Fraschini company of Milan was one of the most progressive of early luxury car manufacturers. It created the first series-built car with four-wheel brakes and was the first to offer straight-eight engines in production. Because of the exceptional quality of the chassis, it was sought after by the wealthy and well known, principally those who wanted a certain amount of flash and glamour as well as elegance. The car shown here was commissioned by Italian-born Hollywood heart-throb Rudolf Valentino, who joined other film luminaries in choosing Italy's finest chassis for personal transport.

Valentino's car, unusually, has a body constructed by the Fleetwood Metal Body Company, a firm set up in Pennsylvania in 1909 for the express purpose of making car bodies. Packard chassis were used for some 80% of Fleetwood production, but Pierce-Arrow, Cadillac, Stutz and Chrysler also used the company, even after the Fisher Brothers, acting for General Motors, bought it in 1925. Fleetwood was known for two attributes: high-quality construction and conservative styling. Clearly an exception in terms of the second, this Isotta is nevertheless exceptionally well made.

At the beginning of the twentieth century, Italian cities were still very independent in the manner of the old city-states. Milan and Turin, the two great automotive centres, were quite separate, and family relationships were of key importance in the industry. Two of the Fraschini brothers and Cesare Isotta were married to the Bianchi-Anderloni sisters, whose brother raced Isotta-Fraschinis, aided by his mechanic, Bindo Maserati. Felice Bianchi-Anderloni in turn created Carrozzeria Touring in 1926, the principal Milanese body builder, which clothed the majority of Isotta-Fraschini chassis, including the few made after World War II. Isotta-Fraschini never resumed full production, and although there have been a few attempts to revive the name, they were without the depth of engineering skill and spirit of innovation and quality that characterized the original company.

above
A menacing cobra rises above the classic IF badge.

opposite
Rudolph Valentino must have cut a wide swathe through Hollywood with this spectacular roadster. The engine-turned bonnet and cowl required endless hours of skilled labour.

opposite

By the standards of the day the cockpit was lavish, although in fact there were few controls, and little extra equipment. The elaborate double windscreen is seen open here.

right

The lithe elegance of the Isotta-Fraschini is readily perceived. The polished bonnet intersects the scuttle, which widens to meet the sides of the cockpit.

On the other hand, there was more
instrumentation than most modern
cars can boast, and every part is
beautifully made. No plastic.

opposite
Every item of body hardware was
beautifully made and perfectly
finished.

1919 HISPANO-SUIZA H6B LABOURDETTE

The brilliant engineer who created the Hispano-Suiza cars, Marc Birkigt, was Swiss, and some of the founding capital was Spanish, but Hispano-Suiza was and is a French company, manufacturer of the finest cars ever made in that country and also of some of the best piston aircraft engines in the world. It was Birkigt who invented and perfected the mechanical brake servo mechanism subsequently used by Rolls-Royce, and who laid down the specifications and details of the splendid straight-six cylinder engine used in this H6B, as well as the smooth-running and powerful V12 used by the company in the 1930s. Hispano-Suiza still exists, manufacturing high-quality aeronautical components.

The 'Hisso' is revered by a coterie of aficionados who know and understand its mechanical qualities, but it is also greatly appreciated for the magnificent coachwork habitually fitted to the elegantly made chassis. The introduction of styling for mass producers by Harley J. Earl at General Motors owes a great deal to Hispano-Suiza. Earl's first production car design, the 1927 La Salle, was no more or less than a careful line-for-line copy of a Hispano-Suiza H6B. That the cars were really quite advanced can be verified by the fact that the Hispano-Suiza Owners' Club regularly stages open-road rallies that attract a dozen or more cars that can integrate perfectly with modern traffic. Ultimate acceleration and braking performance may be modest by current standards, even compared with economy cars, but Hissos can and do run among them without being a hazard or inconvenience to other road users – something that cannot be said for many cars from the same period, even those as expensive and as well respected as the Hispano-Suiza. In its abilities this car was well ahead of its time.

above
The wonderfully incongruous nameplate for the finest French car, citing two other countries, and in Spanish at that.

opposite
Compared to earlier touring cars, the Hispano has bigger doors, access to which was improved by moving the spare wheels and tyres to the back, and the passengers a little further forward.

1924 BUGATTI TYPE 35A

Ettore Bugatti experimented with shapes and ideas for racing cars immediately after World War I. They included a 'streamlined' cigar-shaped racer in 1922 and the notoriously unsuccessful full-width 1923 'Tank' aerodynamic cars. Then, in a sudden return to classicism, he created what many consider his masterpiece: the Type 35 Grand Prix racer. With a vertical wedge at the back inspired by Fiat Grand Prix cars, and his trademark horseshoe-shaped radiator at the front, Bugatti abandoned exotic shapes and built a superbly proportioned and timelessly elegant racing car, probably the most successful of all time and certainly one of the most beautiful. Bugatti would sell any customer the exact specification used by the factory Grand Prix teams. Other car builders kept exclusive use of their latest concepts for themselves, so that only two or three cars in a competition represented the best they could produce. Private Bugatti drivers had a real chance to win races, and many did.

Since Grand Prix cars in the 1920s were two-seaters, the same body and chassis could be used as sports cars, and Bugatti catered to sporting drivers with the Type 35A 'Course Imitation' model – much cheaper to buy, with the same superb handling, but somewhat slower in top speed. The 2-litre engine was simplified and less powerful, coil ignition replaced the magneto, and characteristic flat-spoke alloy wheels with integral brake drums were eliminated in favour of wire-spoke wheels and the brakes of the earlier Brescia model. The 35A was delivered with headlights, but without the mudguards seen here. The basic Type 35 body and chassis fitted with a four-cylinder engine became known as the Type 37, and with a twin-camshaft engine the Type 51. Thus the original 1924 chassis design continued in production into the 1930s, and the cars were still being raced successfully in the 1940s.

above
Standard cars had only the knurled cylindrical radiator cap. The more elaborate fixture above was an accessory item.

opposite
'Imitation' race car it may well have been, but the lines, proportions and details make the Type 35A one of the most desirable sports cars ever offered for sale.

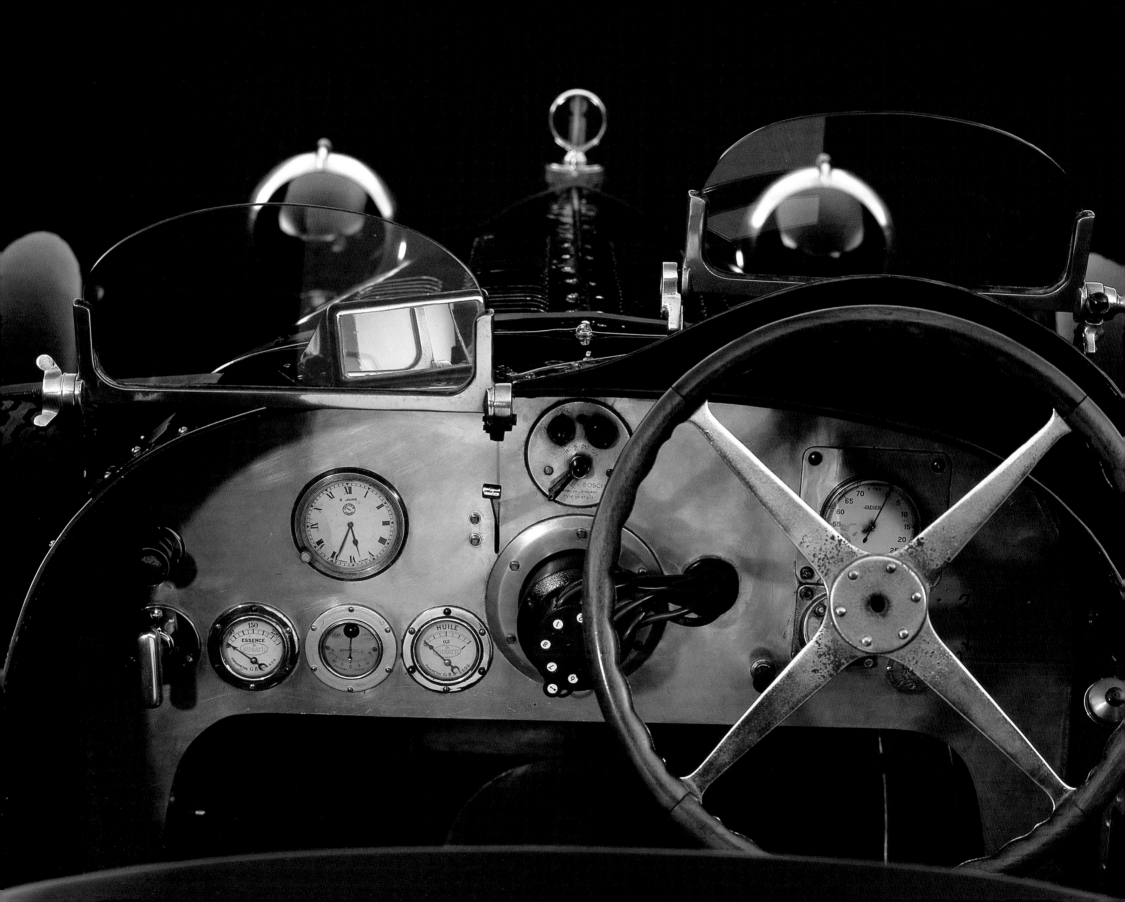

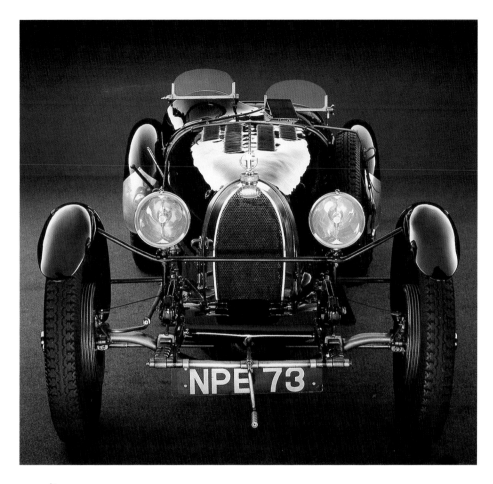

opposite
Coil and distributor ignition was fitted to the Type 35A as an economy measure, but the unit was driven off the back of the camshaft and protruded into the cockpit in the same place as the magneto on the Type 35B racing car. The characteristic four-spoke Bugatti steering wheel and twin aero screens complete a picture of austere efficiency that has its own functional beauty.

above left
The delicacy and elegance of the Bugatti are manifest in this view, the beautifully shaped axle, large brakes and slim radiator attesting to Ettore Bugatti's sense of artistry.

above right
The racing-car tail is somewhat denatured by the cycle-type wings and their supports, but the ensemble is impressive nonetheless.

above
The carefully hand-scraped
tombstone engine block contrasts
with the lovingly curved elements
on the induction side of the engine.

left and opposite
The external details of the body
and chassis are as perfectly
crafted as the internal mechanics.
Everything is exquisitely
proportioned and exactly scaled
to eliminate all excess.

1926 VOISIN C11 LUMINEUSE

When Gabriel Voisin shifted his attention from aeronautics to cars at the end of World War I (he had been an aviation pioneer and built thousands of bombers during the conflict), he sought to apply rigorous thinking to satisfying the requirements of a demanding clientele. In his view a car should be swift, silent, safe and stylish, but always in a logical way. Voisin based his engines on the American engineer Charles Knight's sleeve-valve patents, and they were indeed much quieter than those using poppet valves. They also tended to smoke a little as oil lubricating the sleeves sliding around the pistons burned off, and they were generally less powerful than rival engines of the same displacement. Voisin's cars had great standing, and were used by the president of France and numerous ministers. A born polemicist, Voisin wrote sharp letters to magazines, organizers of competitions and his clients explaining why his ideas were correct and those of others made little sense.

Voisin surrounded himself with gifted collaborators, including André Lefèbvre, a brilliant aeronautical engineer who dealt with chassis and structure, and Noël Noël, who was responsible for the bodywork from 1921 to 1935. But the ideas exemplified by cars such as this Lumineuse were those of Voisin himself. He moved the passenger compartment forward so as to carry all passengers comfortably within the wheelbase, increased the side window area, and placed luggage lockers well forward to assure near-equal weight on each wheel. Voisin's cars were low-built to minimize frontal area, but in the early years he was more concerned about spaciousness than low-drag aerodynamics.

The whole motor industry eventually adopted many of Voisin's ideals, rarely with any acknowledgement of his pioneering work. His spirit of innovation and rationality was transferred to another French marque when he was obliged by the economic crisis of 1929 to let Lefèbvre go and placed him with André Citroën.

Here one sees Gabriel Voisin's determination to make touring agreeable and comfortable. There are luggage lockers behind each front wheel and at the back of the passenger compartment, which is entirely within the wheelbase.

left
Seventy-five years ago there was not much need for bumpers, and Voisin was happy to save the weight they represented.

opposite
Few closed cars offered as much visibility as the Lumineuse. Voisin considered sightseeing an important part of automobile touring.

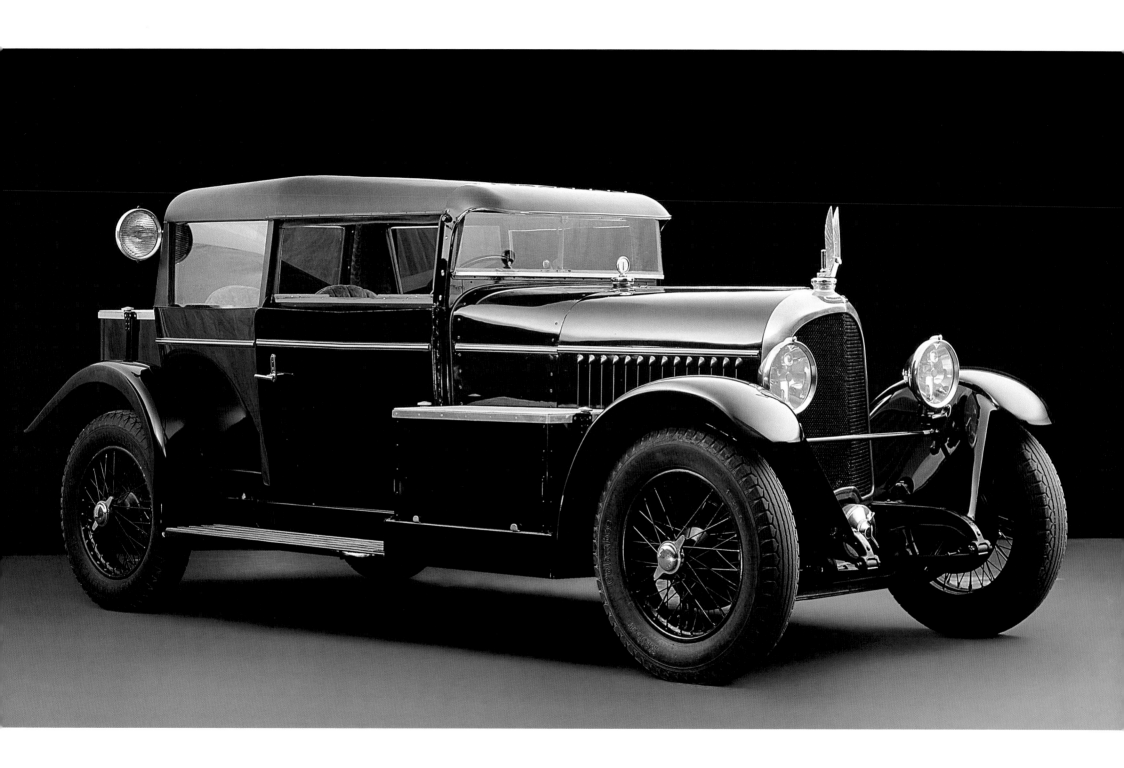

1927 FORD MODEL A ROADSTER

Sales of the two-decades-old Model T had been tapering off to such an extent that Henry Ford simply shut down his factories on 26 May 1927. Fifteen million of the rugged vehicles had been made, but the car that had put the world on wheels had to be replaced. Seven months later the first Model A was on its way to a happy customer. During that production pause Ford moved his assembly line from Highland Park, Michigan, to his new, vertically integrated factory on the River Rouge in Dearborn, where iron ore from the Mesabi Range could be unloaded from Ford freighters, turned into Ford iron and steel, and then transformed into Ford cars and trucks that rolled away on tyres made with rubber from the Ford plantations in Brazil.

Much more conventional in its drivetrain than the Model T, the Model A was a sensation in America, owing in part to the fact that Henry's son Edsel Ford, then President of the Ford Motor Company, believed in design. Edsel saw to it that the bodies were elegantly turned out with belt mouldings pressed into the body sides and pinstriped. Wings were painted in contrasting colours, and some bodies were also two-toned.

In 1929, its best year, the Model A sold to 1,951,092 customers. Altogether Ford made some 4,500,000 Model A four-cylinder cars, then in 1932 offered an eight-cylinder engine in the same chassis for only $10 more than the cost of the slightly restyled Model B four-cylinder model. From 1935 Ford continued to use the Model T- and A-pattern chassis but changed bodies every two years: the deluxe model of one year would become the standard model the next, while new deluxe styling would be developed under the direction of Eugene 'Bob' Gregorie, Ford's first styling director.

After two decades of strict functionality, style came to Ford with the Model A, which was shaped under the direction of Edsel Ford – style the public rewarded with huge sales. Durable and practical, Model As were in general circulation into the early 1960s, when high-speed roads made them irrelevant.

1929 ALFA ROMEO 6C 1750 ZAGATO

At any given time there are typically only two sports-car manufacturers who really matter. Today that pair is Ferrari and Porsche, whereas in the 1930s it was Alfa Romeo and Bugatti. In every era there are, of course, many sports-car builders, and they were far more numerous seventy years ago than they are now. To most connoisseurs, Alfa Romeo was always just that little bit ahead of Bugatti in sports cars throughout the decade of their rivalry. Alfa won Le Mans on four successive occasions (following Bentley's four-in-a-row hegemony at the end of the 1920s), took numerous wins in other sports-car classics, and, by the end of the 1930s, was building the fastest road cars in the world: the supercharged 8C 2900 series.

Of all the Alfa Romeo sports cars, though, the most charismatic and most desired are the 6C 1750 models. Most of the Italian design houses built bodies for the 1750, but Carrozzeria Zagato of Milan created the most delicately proportioned and subtle roadsters. When one looks at the Zagato body, it seems low and sleek, an impression engendered by the fact that the metal skins are perched quite high on the chassis, so that one is unaware of the considerable expanse of mechanism under the painted portions. The cars were designed to be viewed by a standing man, and what went on in pure orthographic drawings was considered unimportant, which implies a far more sophisticated view of psychology than most manufacturers were able to comprehend seven decades ago.

The cars were surprisingly comfortable in terms of ride qualities, despite having the solid axles and cart springs common to most cars of the 1930s. This conferred a major advantage in long open-road races such as the Mille Miglia and the Targa Florio, both of which Alfa won with ease.

The rakish profile perfectly expressed the sporting character of the Zagato roadster. The bodywork is entirely above the wheel centres.

An Alfa driver sat high in the car, and the windscreen is really more a deflector than anything else. Note the rear view mirror on the spotlight.

This is the view that was most
often seen by rival racing drivers
in long-distance races, where Alfa
comfort and handling precision
came into their own.

1929 CORD L-29 CABRIOLET
CORD L-29 PHAETON

The Cord L-29 was a failure, with only 4429 made in its short life between 1929 and 1931. While the US stock market crash of 1929 was to a large extent responsible, the fact that the front-wheel-drive system chewed up tyres and universal joints, the side-valve straight-eight offered mediocre performance and the gorgeous narrow radiator grille caused the cars to overheat with great regularity contributed to its demise. At the same time the design of the low-slung bodies, with their bonnets stretching to infinity and the extremely low overall height, made the cars icons of styling all over the world.

Alan Leamy, then only twenty-six years old, was chief stylist for the Cord car, and the grille, front wings and dramatic 'dishpan' differential cover are attributed to him. American and European coachbuilders created dozens of different bodies, and Cords were consistent winners in European Concours d'Elégance.

Errett Lobban Cord, a high-school dropout, was an extraordinary businessman who got his start in the car industry as a mechanic making cut-down Model T Ford performance cars – a 'hot-rodder' in later parlance. He saved the Auburn company in the early 1920s, repainting and selling some abandoned older cars no one wanted, and then in 1929 went on to create the Cord and Duesenberg marques as part of Auburn. E.L. Cord had an eye for line, and at the apogee of his automotive empire employed some of the best stylists of all time. He knew the value of performance and hired racing drivers to help sell his cars. Indeed, the original configuration of his L-29 was based on Harry Miller's patents derived from his front-drive Indianapolis racers.

Rarely have the big bosses in the car industry truly appreciated design, but Cord built his empire and his reputation on the styling of his cars as much as on their engineering content.

The frontal aspect if the L-29 is marvellous, but there simply was not enough radiator area to cool the Lycoming straight-eight.

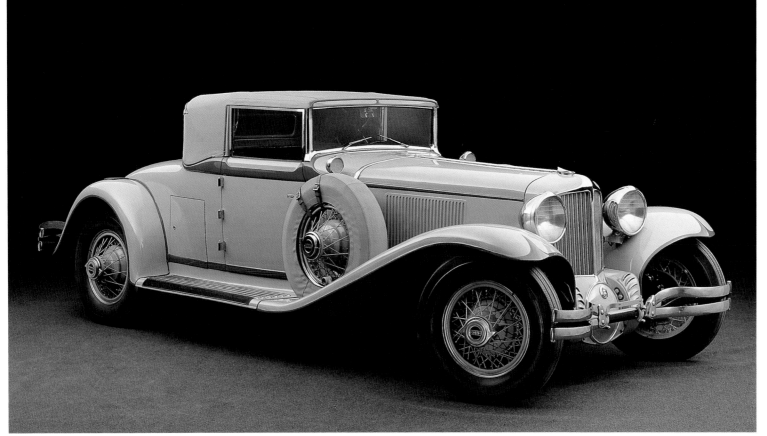

left
The L-29 cabriolet was a
sportsman's dream when it worked
properly. Notice the golf-bag
compartment on the right flank,
and the cooling louvres cut into
the front wing aprons.

below left
The long, sweeping wings are
enormously graceful, a grace rather
spoiled by the parallelepiped roof.

opposite
It is easy to see that the profile
would be far better with the top
folded away, but it is still
impressive.

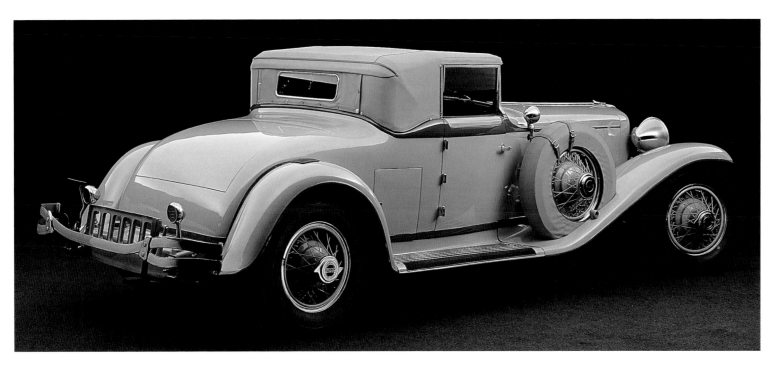

On this 1931 phaeton one can see
the strong visual identity of the
'dishpan' covering the differential.

Apart from the elegant bumpers,
the rear view is typical of the
period.

There is no denying the superb
proportions conferred by the
absence of a driveline to the
rear. If the front-wheel drive had
worked properly ...

The Miller racing car-inspired front
end was impressive, but the L-29
was not a mechanical success.

The iron Lycoming engine put its
considerable weight in the wrong
place. Hillclimbing was at times a
problem for the L-29s.

opposite
Magnificent is the word for the
interior of the L-29 phaeton.
The lavish use of chrome was very
American, and the lack of a gear
stick on the floor very far-sighted.

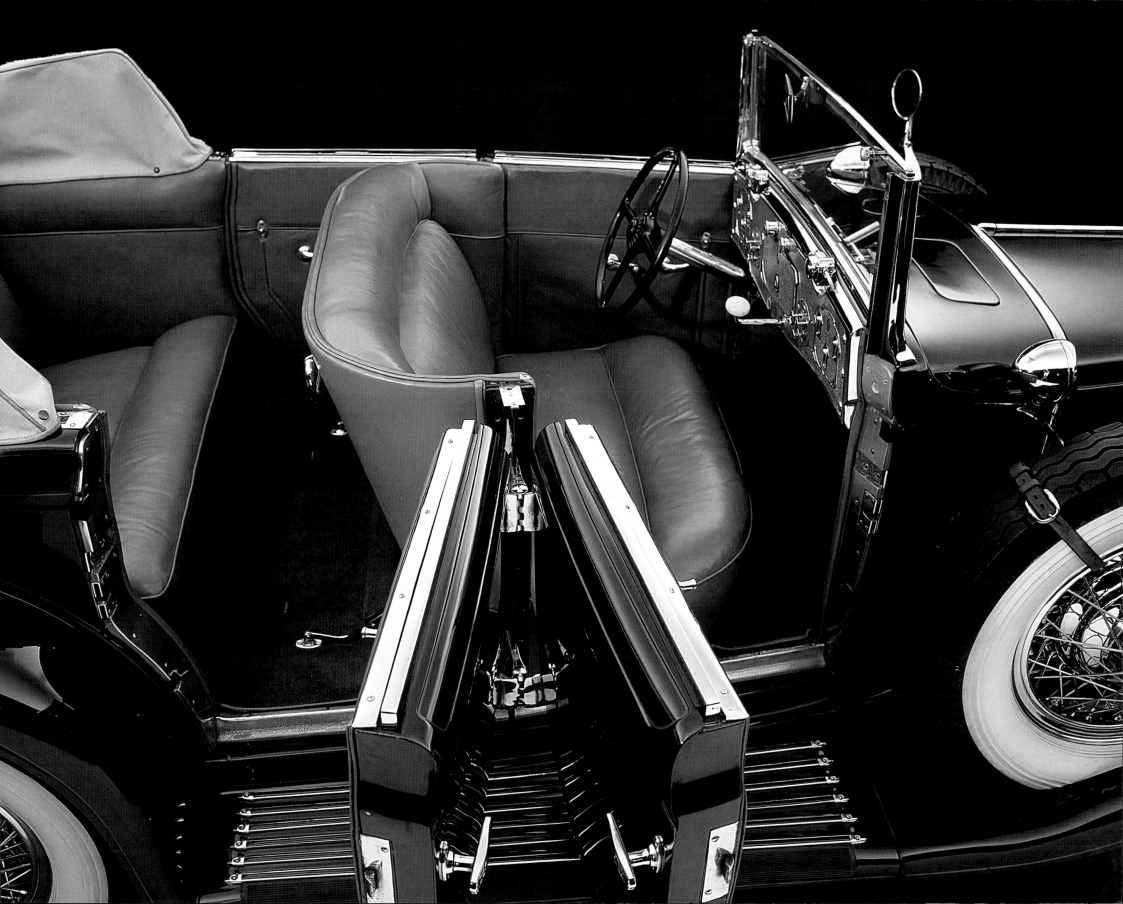

1930 BENTLEY EIGHT LITRE

In the 1920s many luxury car manufacturers were also involved in motor racing, which was often used as a way to prove that cars were a reliable and durable means of transport. Bentley benefited from this form of testing more than any other manufacturer. The French established a 24-hour race for standard touring cars at Le Mans in 1923. Each car was allowed to refill its fuel tank and add oil or water only after having covered a certain distance, and all repairs were carried out using only on-board tool kits. It was a tough concept, but the winning Chenard et Walcker covered more than 2000 km (1240 miles) in the first event. A private Bentley came second, which encouraged Walter Owen Bentley to come back with a factory team the following year. A Bentley won the 1924 race, as did Bentleys in 1927–30.

Worldwide economic depression put Bentley into bankruptcy and the firm was taken over by Rolls-Royce in 1931. It was not to race again for over seventy years. All Bentley designs were scrapped and variations of Rolls-Royce chassis carried the Bentley badge. After its acquisition by Volkswagen in 1998, Bentley re-entered competition, winning the 24 Hours of Le Mans once again in 2003 with the Speed Eight, thus validating the sporting resonance of the Bentley name for a new generation.

This 8-litre chassis does not have particularly sporting lines, although the extremely long, locomotive-like bonnet confirms that the car is extremely powerful. The bodywork is rather formal, as though the intention was to make a limousine but to let it be known that it was a very fast one. The built-in boot is quite modern for 1930 and, given an inclined A-pillar rather than its severely vertical one, this car could easily be a late-1930s design. It is, in any case, an impressive piece of road machinery.

above
Whether they provided as much light as modern lamps or not, those of the 1920s and 1930s were infinitely more impressive to look at.

opposite
The vertical windscreen is behind the mid-point of the wheelbase. The proportions are magnificent, but one has the impression that the car would be diabolical to manoeuvre.

1930 CADILLAC V16 PHAETON

The gruelling worldwide economic depression of the 1930s began with the crash of the US stock market late in 1929. The euphoric prosperity preceding that event led to the car industry investing in ever more lavish designs. E.L. Cord hired the Duesenberg brothers to create a luxury car that was introduced less than a year before Black Tuesday (29 October 1929). Lincoln, Packard, Pierce-Arrow and Peerless in the USA, Maybach in Germany and Hispano-Suiza in France all proposed or were preparing twelve-cylinder cars.

General Motors decided to raise the stakes with a sixteen-cylinder Cadillac, a technically clever thing to do in that it was possible to use the axle and gearbox of the cheaper V8 models, drivetrain components being sized by the torque impulse of one cylinder. A sixteen might have twice as many impulses, but each one was no stronger than pre-existing hardware could absorb. American folklore had it that two Buick cylinder heads were mounted on a crankcase with the cylinders in a 45-degree V. More likely, Cadillac engineers created the whole engine from scratch. It was a beautiful piece of work, with porcelain enamel on the castings and polished-alloy valve covers, and it provided enormous torque and power in relative silence. In the era before automatic transmissions or even synchromesh, it was considered desirable to change gear as little as possible, and the V16 would pull from very low speeds in top gear.

Many coachbuilders provided bodies for the V16, from in-house Fleetwood, acquired by GM-Fisher in 1925, to Battista 'Pinin' Farina (one of his first projects after striking out on his own). Yet no matter who built the body, no matter how elegant or ordinary its styling might be, a Cadillac V16 was a highly impressive motor car: giant of stature, smooth and silent in operation, and very quick for the period.

Imposing and elegant, the Cadillac was quiet and easy to drive – much-desired characteristics at the beginning of the 1930s.

1930 PACKARD EIGHT 7TH SERIES BOAT-TAIL SPEEDSTER

To some traditionalist observers, seeing a boat-tail roadster on a Packard chassis is as incongruous as glimpsing a respectable dowager in a bikini. True, Packard saloons and limousines were typically stately vehicles, but Packards were also very fast, high-performance cars, and the relatively few roadster and speedster bodies made for them were entirely in keeping with the capabilities of the chassis. Packard engineers dealt with wheel tramp, shimmy and other worrisome dynamic problems of early automobiles with considerable virtuosity, and because of their superior chassis engineering and the highly reliable power of Packard engines, many police departments chose Packards as pursuit vehicles.

The Packard reputation alone was enough to inspire many coachbuilders to indulge in overtly sporty lines. There is a delicious contrast between the staid and upright frontal aspect of this 7th Series car and the elegant, sweeping lines of the rear portion of the body, a contrast that had attracted many rich young men in the Roaring Twenties. They could convince their parents that they were sober and responsible citizens by choosing Packard, and still cut a fine figure with their stylish roadsters. Unfortunately, because of their relative impracticality, few sporty Packard cars were preserved, so an example such as the one shown here is rarely seen.

Packard was the one car-maker truly feared by Rolls-Royce, the only firm that consistently maintained standards as high as – or higher than – themselves. There was a strange relationship between the two companies, enhanced when Packard licence-built tens of thousands of Rolls-Royce Merlin aircraft engines during World War II. The last British Rolls-Royce car engine was very much a copy of the post-war Packard V8, as cross-section drawings of the two powerplants confirm. If Rolls-Royce could immodestly proclaim itself "The Best Car in the World", Packard's advertising slogan was even better and more confident: "Ask the Man Who Owns One."

A study in contrasts: staid, respectable front end, rakish and sporty rear bodywork. The quality of construction is self-evident.

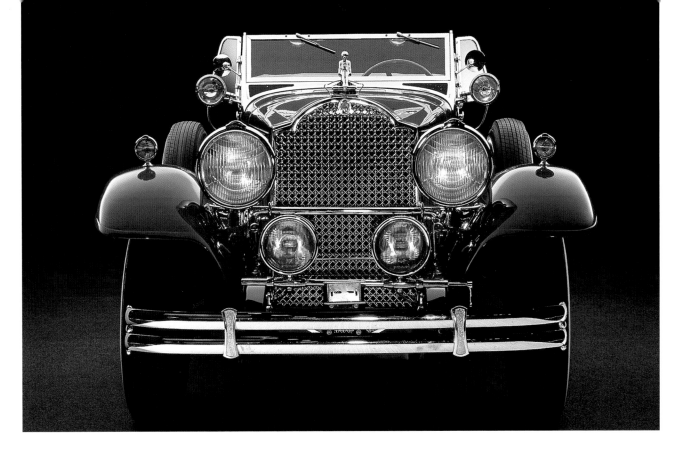

1932 BUGATTI TYPE 55 COUPÉ
BUGATTI TYPE 55 ROADSTER

One of the most beautiful sports cars of all time, Jean Bugatti's Type 55 was an art object in every detail and exerted enormous influence on designers all over the world. Yet only some forty were built, using a collection of essentially surplus components from unsuccessful Bugatti models. Its chassis came from the dismal sixteen-cylinder Type 47 racing car via the equally unsuccessful Type 54, and was mated to the superb engine from the Type 51 Grand Prix car. Some Type 55s had bodies by well-known coachbuilders, but the standard roadster without doors was built at the Bugatti factory in Alsace. The closed coupés are extremely rare, and the one shown here is exceptionally well preserved. The engines are complex and require extensive and expensive maintenance much more frequently than modern cars need a change of spark plugs, but every extant Type 55 is cherished as a work of art as well as a magnificent vehicle to be driven on special occasions and for special events.

A faithful replica of the body style was constructed on a modern chassis by Xavier de la Chapelle in the late 1970s, and it is possible that there were more imitation Type 55s than real ones, but the slightest look beneath the surface reveals the difference. Bugatti cars, of which it is estimated that some nine thousand were built in total, were all truly works of art. Carlo Bugatti, an artist-cabinetmaker from Milan, had two sons: Rembrandt, a celebrated sculptor of animals, and Ettore, whose mechanical intuition led to these wonderful cars. Ettore's eldest son, Jean (Gianberto), seemed to have inherited both his father's sense of mechanics and his grandfather's artistry. Every Bugatti embodies beauty and elegance and is a hand-finished individual art object, a kinetic sculpture.

Exquisite bodywork, Grand Prix car engine and chassis, and outstanding performance made this one of the most desired sports cars of the 1930s.

Type 55 coupés are extremely rare, but a roof and normal doors in no way denature the sportiness of the two-colour bodywork.

Although Bugatti engine
compartments always seem to be
show-prepared, in fact this was the
standard Ettore Bugatti demanded
for all his cars.

The tubular front axle was a
sculpture in itself. All the
mechanical elements of a Bugatti
were shaped to please the eye as
well as to resist external forces.

Like a great cat poised to spring,
the Type 55 always appears to be
ready for action.

As graceful from the rear as from
the front, the car is a symphony
of curves punctuated by the
rectangular windscreen frame.

1932 AUBURN V12 SPEEDSTER

The first Auburn Speedster, introduced in 1928, was a genuinely fast car – guaranteed to do more than 160 kph (100 mph) – and it looked the part, with a boat-shaped tail and wings that hugged the wheels like helmets. In 1931 the car was redesigned by Alan Leamy, who had created the grille, bonnet and front bumpers for the Cord L-29. Leamy kept the running boards flowing off the front wings, but made the wings themselves much longer behind the wheels, bringing the Speedster more into line with the Cord and Duesenberg cars in the Auburn–Cord–Duesenberg stable. It was far sleeker than the 1920s car, but with the Depression at hand such sporty models sold poorly and it was discontinued in 1933. To use up unsold bodies, the company offered the Speedster model again in 1935, putting the old bodies on a newer chassis with completely different wings, no running boards and a higher tapered tail.

To many critics the 1932–33 car was the best of the three iterations because of its classicism and its link with the spectacular Duesenbergs. Great use was made of contrasting colours since it was far cheaper to tape off sections of the body than to make separate pieces of trim. The car shown here is particularly attractive in its cream-coloured trim applied over a bright red.

Auburn was the middle-class, volume-sales member of the automotive empire of E.L. Cord. When he took over it was moribund, yet he managed to make it a real factor in the American market despite a constant lack of finance. Today all three makes are considered to be among the most beautiful cars ever made, but they were all created on miserly development budgets, and often quite elaborate styling was carried out using hand-hammered panels welded together, dedicated tooling being beyond reach. Design, not engineering, triumphed.

above
E.L. Cord always wanted details to be especially beautiful, such as this radiator mascot for the second series of Speedsters.

opposite
The graceful lines do not lie: the Speedster was a very fast car, despite a fairly ordinary side-valve engine.

left
Notice the strong central elements of the bonnet, windscreen and the individual wings. Even in this foreshortened view the car looks fast.

opposite
A Speedster driver had every reason to think himself king of the world in his snug cockpit, surrounded by beautifully shaped details.

1934 CHRYSLER AIRFLOW

Chrysler's radical Airflow is one of the most important cars of all time, at once an incredible engineering success and a crushing commercial failure. Although its architecture, in which the entire passenger compartment was moved forward into the wheelbase, had been pioneered by Gabriel Voisin, the Airflow was the first mass-production example and the first to move the engine forward over the front axle, not behind it. The body was steel-framed and rigidly attached to the chassis, and the overall shape was rounded in front to mimic the aerodynamic qualities of 'streamlined' locomotives of the time.

Applied to both Chrysler and its sister marque De Soto, the Airflow look was not a success with the American public, but it enthralled engineers all over the world, who eagerly copied both the architecture and the appearance. The Airflow concept was picked up by Toyota for its first car, and by Peugeot, Volvo, Fiat and Berliet for production. The VW Beetle is an almost line-for-line copy – apart from the frontal air intakes – of the De Soto coupé.

As it varied so much from the style of the time, potential buyers were reluctant to adopt the Airflow line, which eschewed the long, high engine cover that connoted power and speed. That the Airflow was late into production allowed competitors to mount a whispering campaign that "something was wrong", and a half-hearted restyle for 1935, with a weak imitation of a long bonnet grafted on, did nothing to help sales. Chrysler built Airflows for only four years during the lowest point of the Great Depression, and the car's failure probably put automotive aerodynamics back forty years. The contemporary Lincoln Zephyr had its own VW-like nose altered before production began and enjoyed impressive sales. The Airflow remains the ultimate case study of what happens when good design is mixed with bad styling.

Radical architectural changes brought the engine forward over the front axle and the passenger compartment within the wheelbase. An imposing, inelegant and ultimately unsuccessful masterpiece of design.

right

The front seat of the Airflow was 1.27 metres (4 feet) wide, a huge improvement in comfort. The public did not like the drooping nose, however.

below right

From the rear the Airflow was quite conventional, although the body was wider than in most contemporary cars.

opposite

The interior of the Airflow was incredibly spacious by the standards of the mid-1930s. Tubular seat frames were common elements in several fine cars of the Art Deco period.

1934 CITROËN 11B 'TRACTION AVANT'

One of the most important cars of all time, the Citroën TPV ('Toute Petite Voiture', as it was originally known) was conceived, designed and tooled in only eleven months at the beginning of the 1930s. It was in many ways the prototype for most modern saloons. It had a true unitized body-chassis structure, front-wheel drive, independent front suspension, and reduced overall height – all features that other cars did not achieve for another quarter of a century. Its road-holding was far better than that of most contemporary sports cars, yet it provided very comfortable and spacious transport for five passengers.

The leader of the engineering design team, André Lefèbvre, had previously worked with Gabriel Voisin and brought his background in aeronautical engineering to the world of cars. He went on to create an aluminium monocoque Grand Prix car forty years before Colin Chapman revived the concept in the 1960s for Lotus. The three most important, not to say revolutionary, Citroën cars – this one, the 2CV and the DS19 – all bore Lefèbvre's mark. The styling was the work of Flaminio Bertoni and Jean Daninos, but it is very clearly adapted from the 1932 British Ford Y created by Bob Gregorie, particularly in respect of the radiator shell, which leans backwards and is pointed at the bottom.

The 'Traction Avant', as it is commonly known, existed in several versions. The first was a 1.3-litre 7CV model. The most successful was the 11CV, slightly bigger in all dimensions but still a four-cylinder, shown here in 1951 guise and identical to the first except for vents on the sides of the engine compartment. A 15CV six-cylinder was sold from the late 1930s to the end of production in 1957. A few 22CV V8 prototypes appeared at the Paris Auto Show in 1938, but none is known to exist today. They remain the Holy Grail to ardent Citroën collectors, who refuse to give up hope of finding one someday.

above
The external spare-tyre mounting was an anachronism, belying the design's early 1930s origins. By 1957 the tyre was to be found inside the boot.

opposite
A handsome car even today, the 'Traction Avant' was radical when it was introduced in 1934. This 1951 model varies only slightly in form and detail from the first cars.

From the rear, just another old car, but in 1934 it was a foot lower than almost anything else on the road. The low centre of gravity provided remarkable stability when handling curves.

The business-like frontal aspect was impressive, and the bold chevrons announced the maker in unmistakable fashion. André Citroën began his business career making herringbone gears and wanted the world to know it.

The steering wheel in this late-model 11B is an accessory; most had three-spoke black rubber units. The engine compartment is clean and simple.

1934 BUGATTI TYPE 57 'IMAGINAIRE'

This car, and dozens of others with similar histories, attests to the enormous popularity of classic cars today. This body never existed when its chassis was manufactured. The design was a proposition offered to clients of the Gangloff coachworks in Alsace but never taken up. In 1990, more than half a century after the chassis was made, a Bugatti enthusiast who saw the original side-view sketch – and who had the means – commissioned its construction in a British restoration shop. It is not unique in being rebuilt as something it never was; there are dozens of sporty roadsters and open touring cars with bodies constructed decades after the chassis on which they are mounted. There is nothing intrinsically wrong with this, but it does distort history. In nearly every reconstruction, almost subliminal changes are made, sometimes to 'sweeten' the lines of the body, sometimes to overcome weaknesses in the original conception. That is certainly so in the case of this recreation, which is much rounder in cross section than was common in 1939.

Too many closed cars of genuine interest have been drastically modified, their original bodywork discarded, simply to make them appear higher-current-value sports models. Limousines are converted to open tourers, and long-wheelbase chassis are cut and shortened, not always with proper engineering. Even when the work is correctly performed and the recreation publicly acknowledged, as here, there is a risk that in another half-century the truth will be lost. Gresham's Law applies as well to automobiles as to coins.

With this example every attempt was made to be correct. The chassis owner was able to contact the retired artisan who drew the original sketch at the Gangloff works, enlisted his aid, and acquired a handsome machine as the result. It may well be authentically beautiful, but it is not at all beautifully authentic.

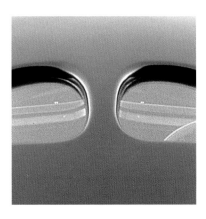

above
Twin rear windscreens were common before curved glass was economically possible, and allowed flat panes to follow the curved contours of a sheet metal roof.

opposite
Radiator grille and lamps are authentic for the period, the twin windscreens considerably less so. A beautiful car, but not a real one.

opposite

More typically Figoni-Falaschi than Gangloff, this oval side window is extremely graceful and elegant.

right

Although the transversely rounded top is atypical for the period, it gives an impression of aerodynamic efficiency and high-speed capability.

below right

The car is so dramatic that it is surprising it was not ordered when first offered. Happily, it was given a second chance.

1935 STANDARD SWALLOW JAGUAR SS90 PROTOTYPE

The work of Bill (later Sir William) Lyons was exceptional. He did not precisely innovate in design, but rather distilled the essence of other people's ideas and transformed them into examples of refined proportion and exquisite line that were a great deal better than the designs that had inspired him. The SS90 prototype was actually rather old-fashioned for 1935, displaying the long, rakish wing lines of some late-1920s sporting cars at a time when French, Italian and even American cars, such as the Lincoln Zephyr, were using teardrop-shaped wings.

One could almost draw the top view of the SS90 with a T-square and compass: the sides are straight and parallel, with three semicircular elements ending the two front wings and the entire rear. This prototype is actually more graceful than the later production SS90 and SS100 models derived from it, particularly in the way the rear curves around the spare wheel. The Englishness of the design is seen in the way that the body sides keep parallel quite far aft, and then sweep around the tyre. An Italian car of the same period typically tapered inward behind the cockpit, approaching the spare wheel tangentially.

Notice the delicacy of the bright metal strips on the after-portion of the front wing, exactly where the feet of entering and exiting passengers will fall. Each is of different length, the angled termination line at the front pointing to the closely spaced bonnet side louvres.

The front of the car is quite different from the rest; it exudes the assurance of an imperial power: upright, rectilinear, massive and confident. Triangulated struts bracing the horizontal headlight mounting bar add a solid geometry to the ensemble, and the increasing fluidity of line as you move backwards recalls the form of a raindrop.

above
Body hardware elements are like pieces of jewellery scattered over the polished surfaces.

opposite
The long, flowing curves of the wings are essentially refinements of 1920s design. Stylistically, the SS90 was obsolete even when new.

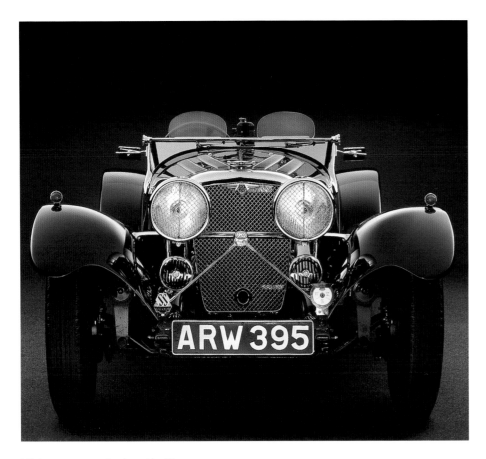

With aero screens in place, the SS
is ready for high-speed running or
racing, although touring was its true
purpose.

Graceful transverse curves make
the car less severe and forbidding
than it might have been. The top
curve of the fold-down main
windscreen is particularly elegant.

opposite
Despite a slightly cluttered and
messy appearance, the cockpit is
nonetheless invitingly sporty.

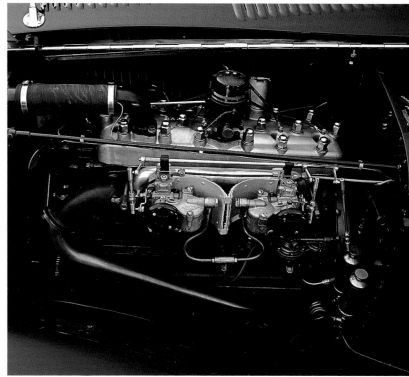

above

The side-valve engine was inadequate for the sporting pretensions of the SS, and was soon replaced for the SS100 model.

left

Despite the plethora of round elements – gigantic headlights, scuttle, and the rearmost curve of the body itself – overall the car is sturdily rectilinear and its sides perfectly parallel.

opposite

Wings taper inwards at the rear, but are exactly parallel to the chassis centreline where they attach to the body.

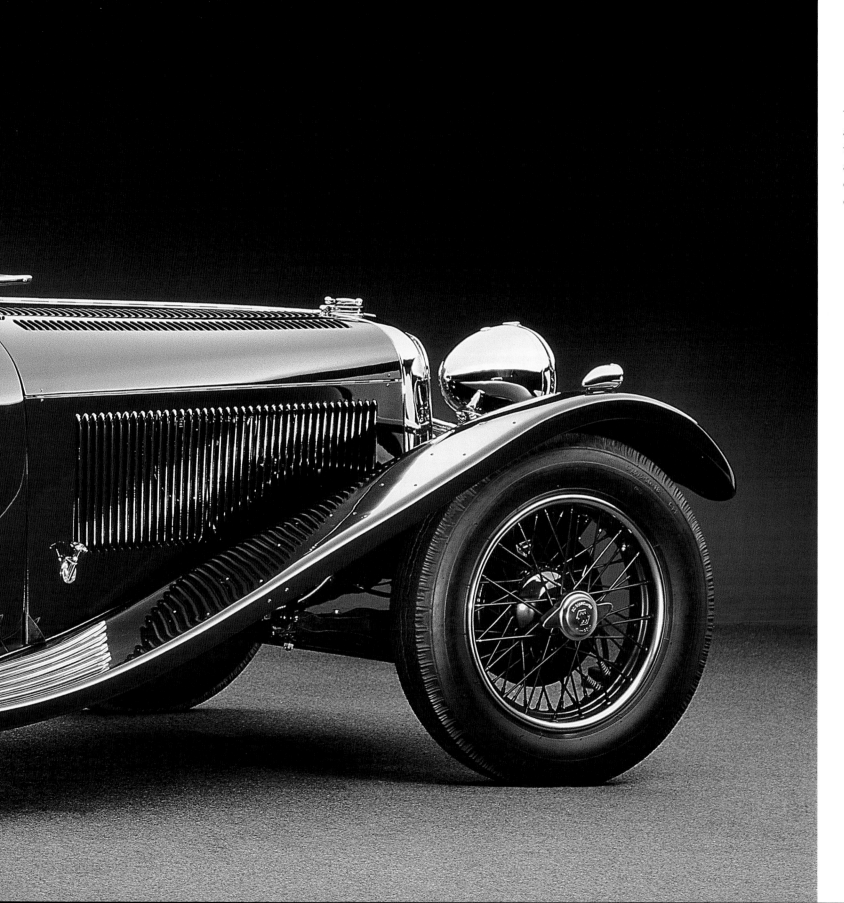

The artful composition of linear and curved elements, the use of functional, bright elements as accents, and the voluptuous sweep of the wings are masterful and completely British in conception.

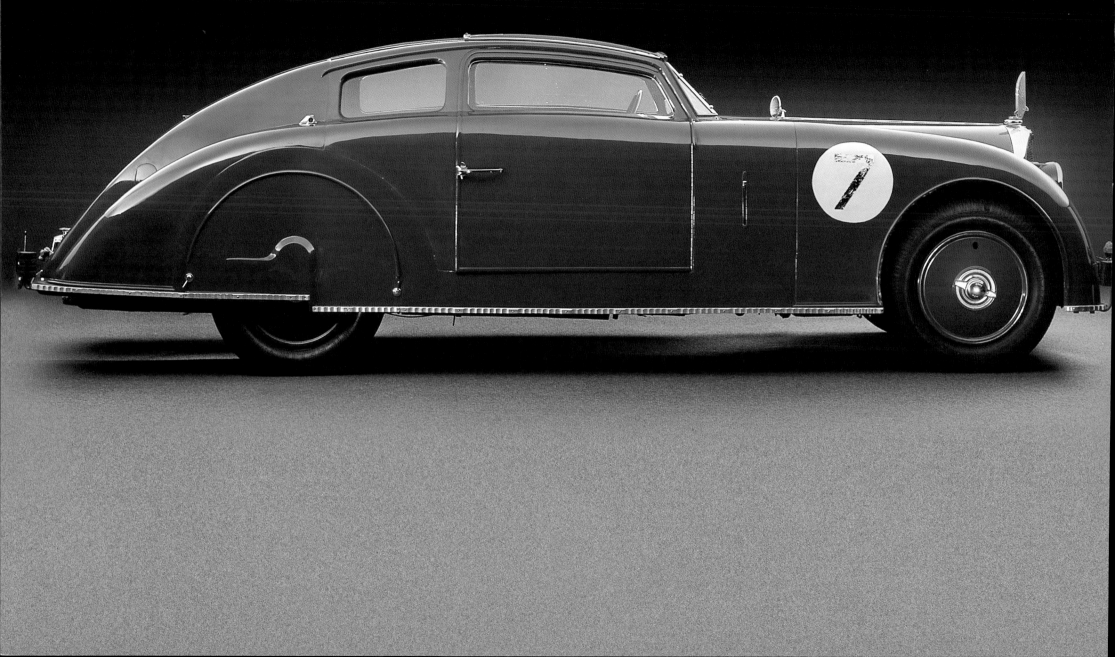

1935 VOISIN C28 AÉROSPORT

Gabriel Voisin was a far-sighted visionary, an inventor and an inveterate tinkerer who became infatuated with the idea of flight early in the twentieth century. He associated himself with Louis Blériot, and when World War I began in 1914 he was in a position to build aeroplanes in great number. After the war he turned away from aviation and devoted his attention to cars, sometimes with amazing results.

One sees in this mid-1930s design most of the attributes of cars built fifteen years later by mainstream manufacturers. The body and wings are integrated in the so-called 'pontoon' form, and great attention is paid to aerodynamic efficiency. The vertical radiator grille was seen as a mark of identity, and both customers and manufacturers were reluctant to see it disappear, although John Tjaarda and Bob Gregorie were already working to change the frontal aspect of cars with their Lincoln Zephyr, the pointed prow of which barely suggested a flat radiator behind it.

Voisin's cars were all characterized by extraordinary riding comfort and exceptional silence of operation – a silence paid for in part by clouds of burnt oil left behind by the sleeve-valve engine. Voisin was early in moving the passenger compartment forwards into the wheelbase, a trend accelerated by the Chrysler Airflow in 1934. Because of their cosseting qualities, the company's cars were favoured by the French president and government ministers, although their custom was not enough to prevent its failure by 1937. Built to uncompromising standards, Voisin cars, like those of many other quality manufacturers, were simply not suited to the strictures of the global economic depression that began in 1929 and ravaged the car industry, leading to the severe consolidation that took place thirty years later all over the world.

The Aérosport profile was resolutely radical. The sleeve-valve engine was decidedly behind the times, however, and demanded aerodynamic refinement for acceptable performance.

Exceptionally advanced for the period, the Aérosport incorporated a fastback body profile, pontoon wings and headlights buried in the catwalks.

Despite the traditional vertical
radiator, the Aérosport was
exceptionally good aerodynamically,
and Voisin raised the catwalks
between wing and bonnet higher
than anyone else had done before.

1936 ADLER TRUMPF RENNWAGEN

Almost totally forgotten today, Adler of Frankfurt was once an important producer of cars, and in its last years it made a number of highly advanced vehicles of outstanding performance. Adler began its vehicle activities with the import of American bicycles in 1880, started to make cars in 1900 and added motorcycles in 1918. World War II put an end to car production, and motorcycles stopped in 1957, leaving the typewriter manufacturing operations (begun, along with car production, at the beginning of the twentieth century) to keep the firm prosperous.

Adler began making front-wheel-drive cars in 1932 using J.-A. Gregoire's patented Tracta universal joints, which were key to smooth performance. More than 100,000 Trumpf Junior cars were made by 1939, five of them racers with aerodynamic bodies based on the theories and research of Hungarian scientist Paul Jaray. A few bumper-equipped *Autobahnwagen* of the same shape were also made and sold. Of the racing cars, only two still exist. The car shown here did not run at Le Mans, but is substantially the same as the cars that won the 2-litre class in 1937 and 1938, taking the Coupe Biennale. In both years the winning Adler finished sixth overall. Apart from featuring front-wheel drive, the Adlers were technically advanced in having very rigid chassis and all-independent suspension. Offsetting that is their low-powered side-valve engines, with only 70 hp available from the 2-litre and substantially less from the 1.5- and 1.7-litre units also used in the 1930s.

Far more interesting than beautiful, the Adler Le Mans cars are significant because of their early adoption of serious aerodynamics research and because the company dared to offer such vehicles for sale. Respected researcher Karl Ludvigsen attributes drag coefficients of 0.23 to 0.30 to the Adlers, figures that are quite respectable almost seventy years later.

above
This exact badge was used on typewriters in the 1950s. Adlers were excellent machines, for both writing and for racing.

opposite
Very few modern cars have as low drag as this elongated form. A remarkable piece of work indeed.

The body sides seem to bulge, requiring straps to restrain them. The surface transitions that separate the front wings are awkward and unnecessary.

The rear body is far more fully realized than the front. There was rear lift, no doubt, but since the tractive force went through the front tyres, it mattered less than with conventional cars.

above and overleaf

The rear three-quarter and side
views of the Adler are the most
dramatic, and also offer the most
convincing evidence of the
intelligence and courage that went
into making it.

1936　BMW 328 ROADSTER

Most automotive historians think of the BMW 328 as the first modern sports car, in that it had independent front suspension for a far more comfortable ride than earlier beam-axle machines, and in that its bodywork more comprehensively covered the chassis and allowed no mechanical elements to be immediately visible, giving a considerable aerodynamic advantage. Although only 464 examples of the 328 roadster were built over a four-year production life, its influence was immense. The engine design, particularly sound with respect to breathing, was claimed, along with drawings and tooling, by Bristol Aeroplane as war reparation and was produced well into the 1950s. BMW 328s were raced and rallied widely, and did extremely well. They won the Alpine Trial, won the 2-litre class at the Mille Miglia, at Le Mans and at other sports-car races.

The handsome styling of the 328 is now credited to one Kurt Joachimson, who, because he was Jewish, received no acknowledgement for his work. Instead it was commonly attributed to a man who joined BMW only after the car was out of production. Joachimson had earlier created the elegant little 315/1 roadsters that first set BMW on the path to its sporting reputation.

Key design elements were the headlights faired into the space between bumper and bonnet, and the leading edge of the front bumpers descending towards the road so that they reduced turbulence (and thus drag) inside the wheelhouses. The body shape is straightforward, but nice use is made of curved separation lines between bonnet and body, and door and body, to add decoration to the simple form. The front wing evolves into a running board that keeps gravel thrown up by the front tyres away from the cockpit and its sharply cut-down doors. Much prized by collectors, a large number of 328s exist today, and parts are still available from BMW.

The bonnet side-vents and leather straps are old-school, but the 328, with its independent front suspension, was a very modern car.

The 328's styling was a nice transitional blend of old and new. Cut-down cockpit sides were pure 1920s, while wing valances and built-in headlights looked to the future.

1936 MERCEDES-BENZ 540K

One of the most beautiful of all cars from the 1930s, and certainly the best German design of the classic period, the 540K Special Roadster chassis had Mercedes-designed bodywork and carried the badge of its home town, Sindelfingen. Opulent curves, lavish use of bright metal trim and slightly oversized body hardware combine to unforgettable effect. The car's proportions, with the radiator well behind the front-wheel centreline, recall an earlier age, but the high waist and roll-up windows make it clear that this is no vintage design, but instead a very sporty and modern (for the period) construction. There were many bodies available on the 540K chassis, but the Special Roadster was the most expensive and today is the most desired of all. Only thirty-six cars were built to this design, although a number of other two-seat convertibles were available on the same chassis.

The straight-eight engine produced 115 hp, but when the supercharger (*Kompressor* in German, hence the K in the model name) was engaged another 65 hp was available, and 180 hp in the 1930s was a towering achievement. The construction quality of the Mercedes was as close to flawless as can be imagined. Take one of these cars apart, and one would find perfectly finished details everywhere. There was, for example, an approved Mercedes method for installing a split pin (cotter pin), and that method was followed in every instance. Very likely no Mercedes cars, before or since the production of the 540K, were so perfectly finished.

That examples of this car change hands today for millions of pounds is fully justified by the extraordinary attention to every detail – as well as by the fact that they are genuinely satisfying to drive, even in modern traffic. The 540K's quality is as apparent in its dynamics as in its magnificent appearance.

Massive, flawlessly crafted and adorned with bright body trim, the Special Roadster was the summation of classic German automotive style in the mid-1930s.

above

Leave off all the brightwork and medallions, and the pure form of the Special Roadster, with its beautiful surfaces and flowing lines, shines through.

opposite

The body hardware of the 540K perfectly expresses the vulgar excesses of the Hitler period, as seen in German dress uniforms of the time.

1937 TALBOT-LAGO T150 SS FIGONI-FALASCHI

Figoni et Falaschi was known for exuberantly flamboyant designs, to the point that some British and American critics referred to the design house as "Phony and Flashy" – a good joke, perhaps, but patently unfair. The cars were also restrainedly scientific. Joseph Figoni was a serious designer who studied aerodynamics and applied himself as much to that discipline as he did to aesthetics, a field in which he was acknowledged as a master. Ovidio Falaschi was an accountant who kept the company solvent – a fair trick in the Depression of the 1930s. From 1936 the firm began to build a series of highly styled, very slippery coupés on Talbot-Lago chassis in two lengths of wheelbase. Some were intended to be grand tourers, but others, on the T150 Super Sports chassis, were outright racing cars in the way that early Ferrari coupés were.

Figoni hated the name '*goutte d'eau*' (raindrop) given to his masterwork by the French press, and instead always referred to the cars as '*coupés américains*', since the first had been built for an American client who was receptive to his ideas about aerodynamics. Other owners included Woolf Barnato, three-time Le Mans winner and former chairman of Bentley, which gives an idea of the stature of the dozen or so cars made to the 'raindrop', or 'teardrop', pattern. The Talbot-Lago chassis was essentially identical to that of the Talbot Grand Prix cars of the period.

A Figoni Talbot *coupé américain* was one of eight automobiles included in the seminal 1951 *Hollow Rolling Sculpture* exhibition at the Museum of Modern Art in New York, and another won Best in Show at California's Pebble Beach Concours d'Elégance in 1997 – an impressive validation for a concept then sixty years old. That so many of the cars survive today is also confirmation that Figoni et Falaschi bodies were exceptionally well made.

Compare the authentic Figoni oval window with the later copy (page 110) to note subtle differences between authentic creation and imitation.

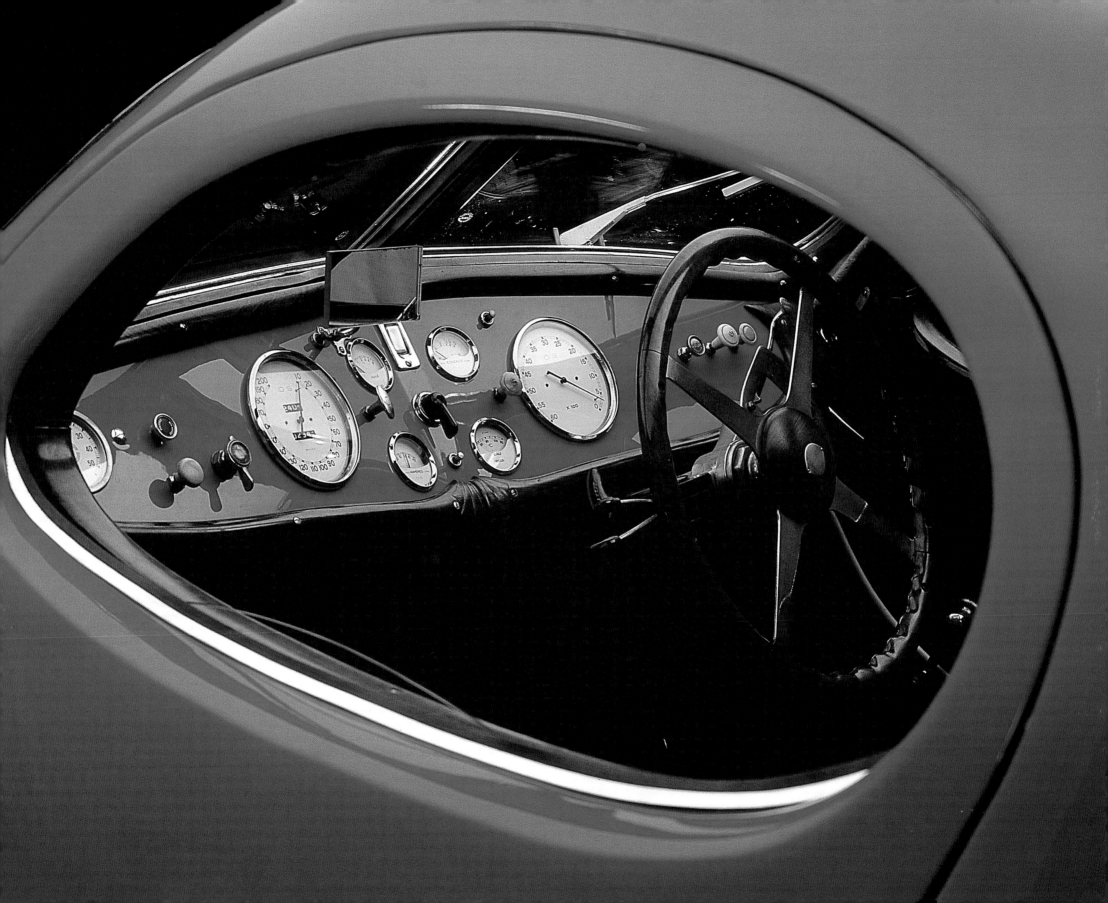

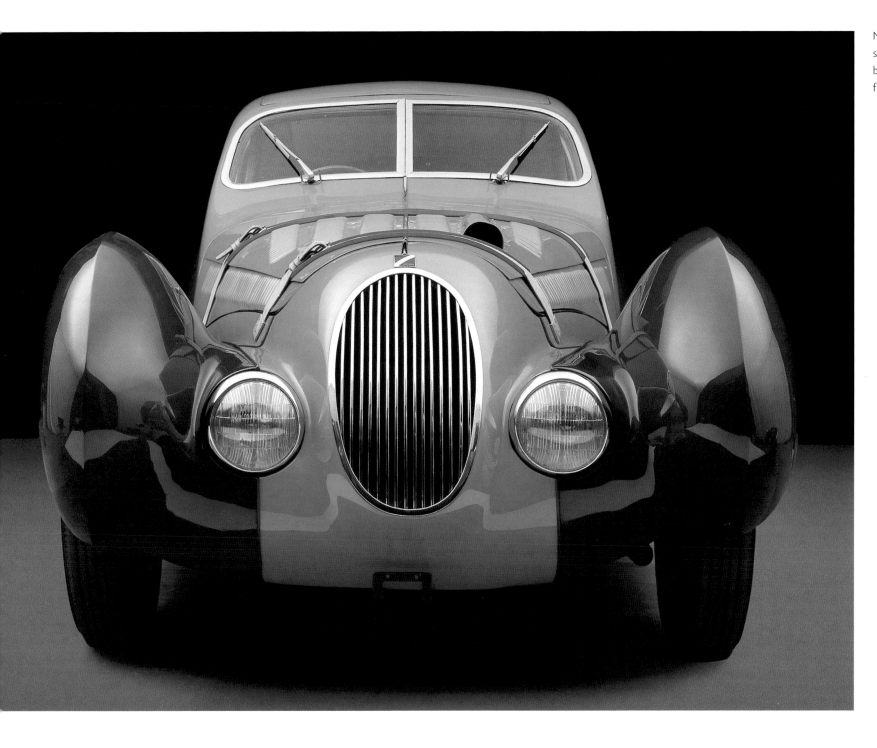

No matter where an air molecule strikes the surface of the 'teardrop' body, it leaves the car in a smooth, flowing path.

Rear-hinged doors make entrance
to the low cabin easy and graceful.
But a loose catch could mean
disaster.

The exquisite forms of Figoni's aerodynamic cars have been cherished for decades, and most examples have been preserved and restored.

1938 CITROËN 2CV

"Four wheels under an umbrella." Rarely in the history of the automobile has a product brief been as succinct and to the point as that for the Citroen 2CV. Pierre Boulanger, newly appointed director-general of Automobiles André Citroën, laid down the rules for "a minimum French automobile" in 1936, soon after taking over the bankrupt company. He specified that the car must carry four people, 50 kg (110 lb) of baggage at 50 kph (31 mph) in comfort, and that a farmer should be able to traverse a ploughed field carrying a basket of eggs without breaking any – and then left his technical people to get on with it.

No beauty, the 2CV – known to generations of French people as the '*deutsch*', and to most of the rest of Europe as '*der Ente*' (the duck) – was, in fact, superbly engineered. André Lefèbrve, the brilliant chief engineer who had come from Voisin, made use of aeronautical practices and built an all-aluminium vehicle. It was ready in 1938, but World War II put an end to the venture before it had been shown to the world. When the car was revived in 1948 in a war-torn France, it was a little more conventional in its materials (steel this time, not light alloy), but it respected the brief perfectly. With two air-cooled cylinders and two fiscal horsepower, the 2CV's engine was indestructible and economical, its suspension was the best in the world, and the cost was low. It was conceived as a farm tool but was instantly adopted by chic Parisians, who probably never removed the doors or put the seats on the ground for picnics, although this was always possible. The appeal was the same as that of today's 4 x 4 off-road vehicles: it signified an attitude. It also did a real job, putting rural people on wheels, and stayed in production for 42 years.

This 2CV from 1959 is virtually identical to the first post-war cars, which varied from the initial 1938 concept in having a steel body. The bonnet still carries the same fine flutes, but the seats are self-framed, not suspended from the roof rails.

1938 VOLKSWAGEN STANDARD

This perfectly original, never restored 1949 Standard, completely without trim or decoration and equipped with cable-operated mechanical brakes, is virtually no different from the hand-made prototypes built in Professor Ferdinand Porsche's Stuttgart home garage in the 1930s.

The shape is well known, the VW Type 1 (also called the 'Beetle' or 'Bug') having been in production longer than any other car. Launched in 1938, it was produced in Germany from 1941 until 1974 and then in overseas factories, with the last, in Mexico, ceasing production in July 2003, so ending a remarkable sixty-two-year run. Less appreciated is the source of the shape. Erwin Kommenda drew the VW plans, but he was clearly inspired by the 1934 De Soto Airflow two-door saloon, an earlier American attempt at an aerodynamic car.

The world knows the Chrysler Airflow well; cars from Toyota, Peugeot, Berliet, Fiat and Volvo were all inspired by the Chrysler four-door saloons. De Soto was a sub-marque of Chrysler, and it had, in addition to its smaller-than-Chrysler four-doors, a two-door saloon that in virtually every line previews the later VW. De Soto headlights were closer to the centre of the car, and it had a grille for radiator air, but the profile of the car and its window and wing forms are the same.

That the VW was a rational design can be seen from the car's long-term success. That its shape was not a styling masterpiece can be seen from its very short life – two years – in service for its creator, Chrysler. VW buyers did not seek style, and did not get it. But they did get an excellent and practical design.

The double-pane rear windscreen was used between 1938 and 1953, but the basic profile remained unchanged until the last car was produced in Mexico in July 2003.

opposite

The austere interior, with its symmetrical instrument panel, remained unchanged until 1953, when the speedometer (the only instrument) was moved in front of the driver.

right

The simple, clean engine compartment changed very little over half a century. An experienced mechanic could remove the engine in fifteen minutes.

1939 BMW 328 MILLE MIGLIA TOURING

One of about half a dozen BMW 328 chassis clothed with aerodynamic bodywork for high-speed races such as Le Mans and the Mille Miglia, this car is particularly significant for the clear influence it had on the Jaguar XK120, which appeared ten years later. One sees every line of the British car, but in a slightly puffy, far less lithe form.

BMW built a few aerodynamic cars to its own designs, but they had none of the elegance of bodies by Carrozzeria Touring, so the Italian house was engaged to create a Le Mans coupé inspired by the racing Alfa Romeo berlinettas it had built earlier. Touring's motto was "Weight is the enemy – wind resistance is the obstacle", and the company lived by its credo. The 328 Touring coupé was outright winner of the 1600-km (1000-mile) Brescia Grand Prix in 1940, which was run on a triangular course between Brescia, Cremona and Mantua, and which replaced the Mille Miglia. The roadsters finished third, fifth and sixth.

There is a certain conservatism in the lines of the roadster – and in the Jaguar inspired by it – in that the front and rear wings are kept clearly separate. Certain other aerodynamic cars of the period, and specifically the winning BMW Touring coupé, had pure pontoon forms, with no separate indication of front and rear wheelhouses.

This car, now more than sixty years old, represents very well the constant tendency towards multinational convergence in car design. The BMW chassis is pure German, but the cylinder head of the six-cylinder engine was copied, detail by detail, from a French car – the Talbot Type 150 Sports presented at the Paris salon in 1935 – using a 1921 Georges Roesch patent. The bodywork was wholly Italian and the best application of the design was British.

No, not a Jaguar XK120, but definitely the inspiration for it. This is the most conventional of several Mille Miglia cars built by Carrozzeria Touring for BMW.

above

The 2-litre six-cylinder engine had an unusual cylinder head, which was inspired by the patents of a Swiss engineer. Carburettors sit on top of the head, which makes the engine quite tall.

right

The moulded-rubber steering wheel seems rather anachronistic but was quite standard for all but the most expensive cars of the time.

opposite

Quite a beautiful car for any period. Only the tiny rear lights give away the age of this one-of-a-kind roadster.

The minute door is a little absurd, but it was only required for the rulebook, not for the driver's ease of entry.

1940 WILLYS JEEP

Arguably the best-known car in the world, the humble military General Purpose quarter-ton truck, known as the Jeep, was created by America's Bantam company in 1940. Demand was greater than Bantam could supply, so the design was licensed to Ford and Willys-Overland. The latter made by far the greatest number of units and contrived to hold on to both design rights and the name 'Jeep' after the war.

Dwight D. Eisenhower cited the military Jeep as one of the three most important items of military hardware in World War II (the others being the bulldozer and the Douglas C47 cargo plane). Extremely simple and extraordinarily robust, the Jeep was indispensable. Basic wartime models continued in production in the 1940s as the Civilian Jeep (CJ). When a taller power unit replaced the side-valve engine, the bonnet was raised. The CJ chassis stayed in production in the USA until the 1980s, and versions of the original design are still in production in India.

The 1944 example seen here is a carefully restored collector's item, but hundreds of original 1940s Jeeps are still in use as work vehicles all over the world. Easy to drive, easy to repair and incredibly strong, the Jeep is enormously attractive to users in the Third World.

Willys introduced a line of Jeep-shaped passenger vehicles on a longer wheelbase in 1946. The Jeepster, an open four-place tourer and a station wagon version – surely the first of what are today called Sports Utility Vehicles (SUVs) – joined the Jeep. Jeep-brand all-wheel-drive vehicles have been in production for more than sixty years, and promise to continue for decades to come. Jeeps were made under licence in Brazil, France, Japan and the Philippines. It is little known that even the Land Rover prototype was built on a Jeep chassis.

above
Faithfully reproduced military markings are correct for this 1944 Jeep, now a treasured collector's item.

opposite
Possibly the best-known automotive form in the world. Although Volkswagen has built tens of millions more vehicles, the Jeep has been everywhere, in every country on earth.

It would be difficult to imagine a simpler frontal design than this. The blocks on the leading edge of the bonnet receive the windscreen when it is folded.

Functional simplicity again, with extra fuel can, spare wheel and tow bar ranged across the back. The buttresses beneath allowed Jeeps' front bumpers to touch when the vehicles were tightly packed in ships or aircraft.

opposite
As with early British sports cars, the Jeep top is more an affectation than functional when it comes to keeping off the rain. But it did make an excellent sun shield.

left
There were not many American boys in the 1940s who could not repair a Jeep with only a few simple tools. It was crude, but robust and simple.

opposite
The very definition of functionality – perhaps more direct even than a racing car cockpit, which did not need to make provision for an infantryman's rifle.

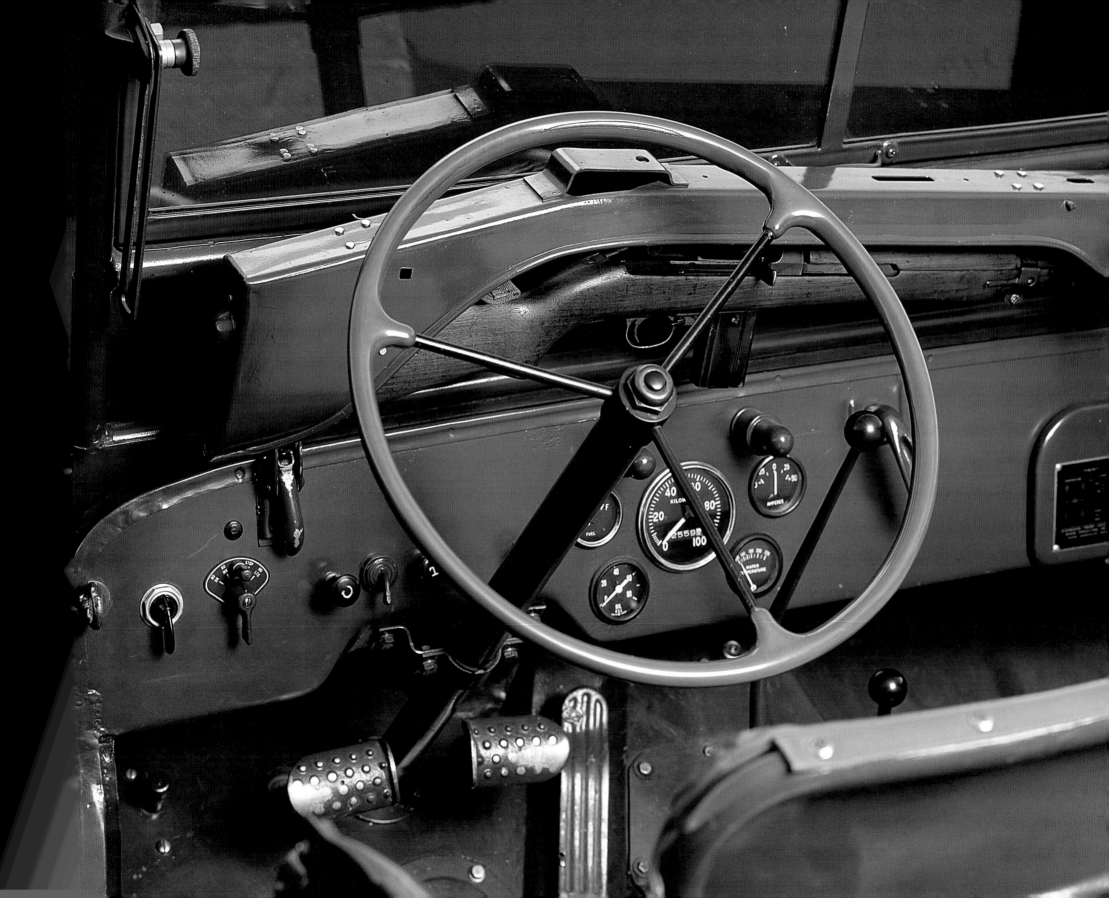

1947 CISITALIA 202 PININ FARINA

Given that only 170 Cisitalia 202 chassis were made in the 1940s and that some of those were prototypes, racing cars and cabriolets, it is astonishing that the coupés have had such an enormous influence on car design. The vehicle shown here is part of the permanent collection of the Museum of Modern Art (MoMA) in New York, the first car to be so honoured. This particular example is the Pinin Farina prototype, exchanged by the Turin coachbuilder for another coupé that the museum had owned previously. (This switch might have been inspired by the fact that MoMA's first car was not made by Pinin Farina.) Some Cisitalia 202 coupés were made by Alfredo Vignale, who had built the prototype racing coupé, and some by Stabilimenti Farina, which was owned by Battista 'Pinin' Farina's elder brother, Giovanni.

The characteristic front end, all the way back to halfway through the doors, was designed by the aeronautical engineer Giovanni Savonuzzi, Cisitalia's technical director, for a racing coupé that ran in the 1947 Mille Miglia. Pinin Farina (whose family name was changed to Pininfarina by presidential decree in 1961) simply widened the rear roof and added vestigial rear wings, thereby producing a masterpiece of car design with his wonderful sensitivity to form and sense of style and proportion. Pinin Farina gave the production coupé a magnificent interior featuring corduroy fabric for the seats and painted sheet metal for the instrument panel.

The lovely flattened-bottom oval grille owed its existence, as did the elegant tubular chassis, to the fact that Cisitalia's founder, Piero Dusio, owned the Beltrame bicycle factory, which had a stock of small-diameter steel tubes. Savonuzzi simply bent small tubes and welded them together to make the grille, while Fiat's Dante Giacosa made the chassis also from those on-hand materials.

The key design of the post-World War II period, the Cisitalia was created first by Giovanni Savonuzzi for racing, then civilized by Battista 'Pinin' Farina, who shaped everything from the middle of the door to the tail end.

And everything here, apart from the headlight rims, was designed by Giovanni Savonuzzi.

1949 CHEVROLET FLEETLINE TWO-DOOR SEDAN

Chevrolet was the best-selling marque in the world at the end of World War II, with its 1946–48 cars based on pre-war body tooling. The 1947 Cisitalia with its applied rear wings strongly influenced all of General Motors' post-war designs, beginning with Cadillac and Oldsmobile models in 1948. Ed Glowacke's design for the 1949 Chevrolet drew from the same source but simplified details to suit the low price. Chevrolet offered a wide range of body styles for 1949, including both fastback Fleetline and notchback Styleline two- and four-door sedans along with coupés, convertibles and station wagons. More than one million Chevrolets were sold in 1949, most of them the conventional Styleline sedans, since the American public never warmed to the tapering aerodynamic shapes of the Fleetlines.

One group that did find the two-door Fleetline appealing was the design team at H.J. Mulliner, coachbuilders to Rolls-Royce and Bentley. While the Bentley R-Type Continental cost nine times more than a Chevrolet Fleetline two-door sedan and was probably more than ten times as refined, its body shape is definitely lifted from the cheap American car, only the inboard headlights and traditional grille varying greatly.

It is safe to say that only the styling of the Chevrolet was up to date at the end of the 1940s. The basic chassis design was pre-war, as was the simple cast-iron 3.5-litre engine, launched in 1929 and last revised in 1937. Body shapes were the same for 1949 and 1950, with tiny changes in chrome trim, and the 1951–52 Chevrolets simply had longer and higher rear bumpers, as did the 1952 Bentley. Surface modelling of the tapering rear roof was virtually flawless, and even today American hot-rodders continue to base completely modern vehicles on their body shells.

The roof shape and the rear wings are strongly influenced by the Cisitalia 202. The front end, with its high bonnet, is typically American.

Taller, fatter, but definitely inspired
by the Cisitalia of Pinin Farina.

opposite
Americans found this post-World War II
popular car design from General Motors
tremendously luxurious.

A dollar grin for the American masses.
The only difference between this 1950
car and the original 1949 model are
the ribs on the vertical bar under the
parking lights.

1949 JAGUAR XK120

The XK120 was an astonishing tour de force for Jaguar when it appeared at the end of the 1940s in a country still suffering the privations of wartime long after victory had been declared. The engine, Jaguar's first design, had all the features of the most noble engines of the past: twin overhead camshafts, a crankshaft bearing between each cylinder, individual ports for each cylinder – whatever engineers imagined during long nights of fire watches during the war was incorporated. The 3.4-litre capacity gave 160 bhp, an unheard-of figure at the time, and the performance – it was the fastest road car ever offered for sale in Britain – excited a nation living a grey, rationed life. It excited other nations as well, particularly when a 'standard' XK120 was driven to a measured 213.4 kph (132.6 mph) on a yet-to-open motorway in Jabbeke, Belgium, in 1949.

Hollywood took to the XK120 in a big way: Humphrey Bogart and Clark Gable were among the stars who bought them. Nothing on the road was more dramatic than the XK120. The car shown here, now part of a Swiss collection, was Gable's. The present writer rode Los Angeles public transport for two hours to take a look at it, but was repelled by an imperious salesman. "Oh, I think he can take a look at it. I just bought it," said a deep voice, as a small, smiling man came around the corner of the showroom. "Hi, I'm Clark Gable. Would you like to sit in it?" Imagine the impression that made on a boy too young to drive, but realize that the car itself was even more impressive.

More than anything else, the XK120 established Jaguar as a world marque. At its wheel drivers such as Stirling Moss and Formula One world champion Phil Hill showed what it could do. It was, and is, a masterpiece.

The XK120 was an exceptionally handsome roadster that captured the world's imagination at the end of the 1940s.

1952 BENTLEY R-TYPE CONTINENTAL

If the 1949 Chevrolet Fleetline was an extremely good-looking car with mediocre mechanical elements and build quality no better than average, the Bentley R-Type Continental, which reprised most of its overall form, was its opposite: an exceptional car with the finest construction known to the car industry at the beginning of the 1950s. It was hand-built, a monument to traditional coachbuilding skills. Certainly the fastest four-passenger car in the world at the time, it offered the silence and smoothness expected of a Rolls-Royce product and a distinguished presence recognized everywhere, along with a hint of the original Cricklewood Bentley tradition of very high performance.

The cross-fertilization of body design is far more common than most observers realize, and it usually – as here – has a positive effect. No one looking at this H.J. Mulliner Bentley could imagine it to be an American car; there are too many clear marks of identity that stamp it as British and as a Bentley, if only details such as the extremely long door handles, which were created to be beautiful but were not cheap. At the same time there is nothing about the overall form and volume of the Continental that has any antecedents in British car design before 1952, so it is both natural and reasonable that the Mulliner designers should have sought inspiration outside the bounds of domestic practice. From the front-wheel centreline to the rear, the Continental is clearly 'inspired by' the Chevrolet; from there forwards it is strictly traditional; and yet the whole is quite beautiful and absolutely coherent.

On its introduction it was the most expensive car on offer, analogous to the Mercedes-Benz Maybachs, BMW Rolls-Royces and Volkswagen Bugattis that come on to the market today. Unlike those German British cars, the R-Type Continental was the real thing, requiring no explanation or rationalization. It was the best.

The world's fastest and most expensive four-passenger car in the early 1950s, the Bentley R-Type was also very beautiful.

The frontal aspect of the R-Type
Continental was quite traditional
and bore a close relationship to the
R-Type saloon.

opposite
This is the view that other road
users would have seen as the Bentley
swept by.

The rear is completely different from
any earlier British car, but notice the
parallel sides of the boot lid (a national
characteristic). The fins on this 1954
model are pronounced.

1952 FIAT 8V GHIA

One of the most curious cars ever offered for sale by a major manufacturer, the 8V was built in only 114 examples over a three-year period – surely a costly exercise. It is possible that another hundred cars using the same 2-litre V8 engine were made by Siata, a Fiat subsidiary company devoted to tuning Fiats and making special series with individual bodies.

In standard form the 8V was quite awkward, but a few chassis were fitted with coachbuilt bodies, of which this Ghia coupé is an excellent example. Carrozzeria Ghia called the style 'Supersonic', and built versions on the chassis of several manufacturers, but the size of the 8V chassis made it perfect. The design influenced many other cars. The Volvo P-1800 derived much of its shape from Ghia, Chevrolet recapitulated the side 'boom' on 1958 models, and tens of thousands of Volkswagen Karmann-Ghia coupés used the Supersonic's roof shape.

The name '8V' came about because Fiat lawyers were convinced that 'V8' was a proprietary Ford label. It was not, but the legalists could convince themselves that they had done something clever in changing the nomenclature. The Fiat engine had the unusual V-angle of 70 degrees, which imposed balance problems avoided in the more conventional 90-degree layout. Despite that, the 2-litre engine was quite large, as wide as the 4.3-litre Chevrolet V8 engine that appeared in 1954.

From its proportions, one expects this to be a big car, but in fact an optical illusion is generated by the very small size of the upper body and roof. One sits quite low, with feet extended forwards under the scuttle; the boot is minuscule; and a good part of the long nose overhangs the front wheels. The bumperless form represents the triumph of style over practicality.

That sign on the nose says 'Otto Vu', not 'V8', according to Fiat. A small car, the Ghia 8V is nevertheless imposing and seems bigger than it really is.

The surfaces of the Ghia body are complex and incredibly difficult to make, a fine tribute to the craftsmen who built the car.

opposite
Italian designers became proficient in using chrome in cockpits during the 1950s and created masterpieces of elegance with seeming ease.

1953 STUDEBAKER CHAMPION STARLINER

Studebaker was the USA's oldest car company when this car arrived, having been in the animal-drawn vehicle business for more than a hundred years. Some of the Conestoga wagons used for the trek to the American West were Studebakers. The company's fortunes waxed and waned, but at the end of World War II it was the most successful of the 'independent' car manufacturers in America (that is, those not tied to the 'Big Three': General Motors, Ford and Chrysler). Studebaker had built a light car in 1939 that was moderately successful and immediately after the war was one of the first companies to launch an all-new vehicle. Raymond Loewy's design firm acted as Studebaker's styling department and it produced great results. The 1947 saloons influenced the whole industry with their flat sides, add-on rear wing shape and curved-glass panoramic rear windows.

This 1953 coupé, intended to be only a show car when it was first proposed, was a masterpiece. It was lower than any other American car, long, svelte and beautifully detailed by Bob Bourke, one of Loewy's chief lieutenants. It was exceptionally efficient aerodynamically, to the point that hot-rodders have been able to run stock-body Studebakers close to 483 kph (300 mph) at Bonneville Salt Flats, with the only change being the removal of the visors over the headlights – and the addition of hundreds of horsepower, of course. That the car was influential can best be seen in the Citroën DS19, which has all of the Studebaker's lines superimposed virtually one for one on to the 1934 Traction Avant mechanical package.

Unfortunately, one great design in a model range consisting mostly of less attractive saloons and station wagons is not a recipe for enduring success, and declining sales forced Studebaker into a merger with moribund Packard in 1954. Studebakers were always solid products, and at least one model, the Starliner coupé, was a high point of American car design.

above
Not exactly a Mercedes emblem, but closely related. Studebaker distributed Mercedes cars in the US for a time.

opposite
This was a tremendously influential design: many of its characteristics and lines showed up later on other cars, including French and Italian makes.

American designers sought to make cars
look as long as possible. Here, the wing
line is extended in front by visors over
the headlights and in the rear by tail
lights leaning rearwards at the top.

184

right

Masterful simplicity. The twin grilles stretch the full width, the bumper is straight and wide, and the air intake is beneath it.

below right

Reflective disks on the rear bumper were added to suit European licensing requirements and should be ignored as one admires the artful composition of diverse elements.

1953 CHEVROLET CORVETTE

The first car to be put into production with a so-called 'plastic' body, the fibreglass-bodied Chevrolet Corvette was first shown to the world in January 1953 as a 'dream car' in the General Motors Motorama show in the Grand Ballroom of the Waldorf Astoria Hotel, New York. In every way, except for styling and its American-sized overall width, the Corvette was a copy of the Jaguar XK120. From the seating package to the use of a 3.5-litre in-line six-cylinder engine, from the 102-inch wheelbase to the specification of clip-on side curtains, the Corvette aped the charismatic Jaguar, well known to Americans for its speed-record runs in Belgium and its adoption by Hollywood film stars.

Only six months after being proposed as an unobtainable "car of the future", the Corvette was put on sale in June 1953. Available only with a definitely non-sporting two-speed 'Powerglide' automatic transmission, the Corvette was scorned by sports-car aficionados for its lack of purity, and by enthusiasts because it was, in fact, rather slow.

Only a few hundred Corvettes were assembled in Flint, Michigan, during the second half of 1953, all of them white with red interiors, but production continued in a dedicated factory in St Louis, Missouri, in 1954, with a few hundred more cars turned out, still with the three-carburettor six-cylinder engine and automatic gearbox. In the autumn of 1954 Corvettes became available with a new 4.3-litre V8 engine, extremely cheap to manufacture and a marvel of efficiency – so much so that the basic engine architecture continues in production today, fifty years and more than 90 million units later. Restyled several times, the car gained displacement and power to become a real performer. Known to Corvette enthusiasts as the C-1 series, the 1953–62 Corvettes are highly prized by collectors today.

The first Corvette was shown as a 'dream car' at the Motorama in January 1953. In June, production versions were available for purchase with no change from the concept.

The Motorama design continued
in production for three years. This
example was built in 1954, still with
the original 3.5-litre 'Blue Flame Six'
engine and two-speed automatic
gearbox.

right
Jet-exhaust tail lights reflect the general fascination with jet aircraft in the 1950s.

below right
The toothy grille was a Harley Earl favourite and was preserved for seven years in one form or another. Otherwise the car was very clean and simple.

1954 FERRARI 375 MILLE MIGLIA PININ FARINA

To many observers, this is one of the greatest of Pinin Farina's designs. Created as a racing car, with all the functional aerodynamics implied by that purpose, it is also supremely elegant in form, a true grand-touring car. In the mid-1950s no high-performance car had air conditioning, so the car bought by a playboy for quick trips from beach resort to ski lodge was no more lavishly equipped than a racer.

Farina was experimenting with forms here. Notice how the front wing graduates from the perfect circle of the headlight, set behind a plastic shield to protect the glass lens, to a triangular section from the wheel centreline rearwards. This bevel reduces frontal area; not by much, but enough to matter, and the result is a beautifully controlled highlight along the body flank. As a weight-reduction measure the glass area is minimized, and the windscreen takes an unusual form: straight and horizontal across its top, dropping down at the outside edge of the scuttle. The two-piece windscreen was appropriate for racing, being easier and cheaper to replace should gravel break one part.

The rear wing form stands only slightly proud of the body surface and begins with a straight line at the rearmost edge of the door. In typical Italian fashion the bottom of the body on the sides is higher than the chassis, and the lower part of the nose drops well below that level, smoothing airflow at the centre of the front end. The front-end peak is just at the level of the headlights. Proportions and stance are visually perfect, if not actually so. We know now that 'motorboat' front ends like this tend to cause lift at very high speeds – and the 375 Mille Miglia could do 266–74 kph (165–70 mph) flat out – but it looks absolutely wonderful.

Despite its evident elegance, this car was not made for grand touring. It is purely and simply a racing car.

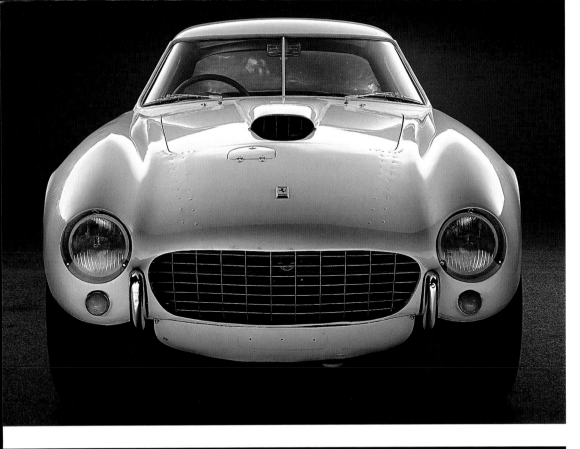

left

Beauty and efficiency in one
package, optimized for the mad
1000-mile dash around Italy that
was the Mille Miglia.

below left

The simple forms of the racing body
made it easy and quick to build. The
Farina design was probably executed
by Carrozzeria Scaglietti in Modena,
close to the Ferrari factory.

opposite

In all his cars what really mattered
to Enzo Ferrari was the engine,
and the best of them were always
twelve-cylinder units such as
this one.

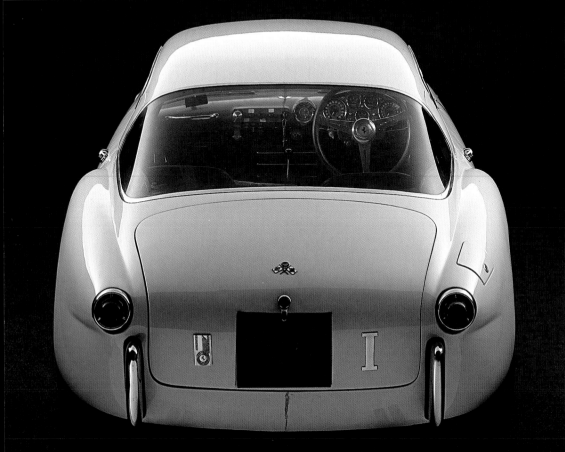

1954 MERCEDES-BENZ 300 SL

An extraordinary car, made by hand in quite small numbers (1374 over four years), the 300 SL was the symbol of German industrial resurgence after the devastation of the Hitler years. In the aftermath of World War II Mercedes resumed production of pre-war designs that seemed hopelessly old-fashioned in the light of American exuberance, and its first modern cars, the 180 and 220 saloons, were essentially shaped as copies of stuffy, style-free late-1940s Dodges with a traditional upright Mercedes grille added. So the spaceship shape of the racing 300 SLs in 1952–53 was astonishing. Mercedes won the 24 Hours at Le Mans, the world's most important sports-car event, in 1952, and there was immediate interest from America.

New York-based, Austrian-born entrepreneur Max Hoffmann told Daimler-Benz that he was prepared to buy 1000 road-going versions of the racing cars for distribution in the USA, and in 1954 the definitive production version was presented. If the roof shape and characteristic gull-wing doors of the racing cars were retained, the lower body was considerably revised. 'Eyebrows' over the wheel openings allowed the body to be narrowed considerably while retaining the same wheel track, enough trim was added to civilize the car, and there were proper bumpers, which were missing from competitive Italian cars of the period.

One of the bumps on the bonnet provides clearance for the fuel-injection manifold; the other is simply there for the sake of symmetry. Subtle shaping of the chrome mouldings, grille surrounds and light bezels gave the 300 SL an impression of solidity and strength, but it went against typical German design in that it looked light and graceful, more like an aeroplane than like a tank. It was at once elegant and serious, and re-established the Mercedes name in North America.

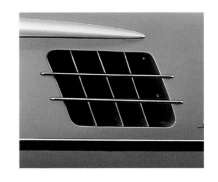

Giving the air intake a slightly trapezoidal form helped immensely in transforming the 300 SL racers for road use, as did the adoption of the company logo as the principal grille element.

above
Roof-hinged doors were a stroke of genius from the point of view of style, although their original purpose was to allow sufficient space to enter above the high, wide sills. The result was much copied but never equalled.

right
Flow-through ventilation outlets on the roof helped make the cabin comfortable. Luggage space behind the two seats and in the long, shallow boot made touring practical in what was a sublimated racing car.

opposite
Access to the tight cockpit could be improved by flipping the bottom of the steering wheel forward while climbing in in order to increase space for the legs.

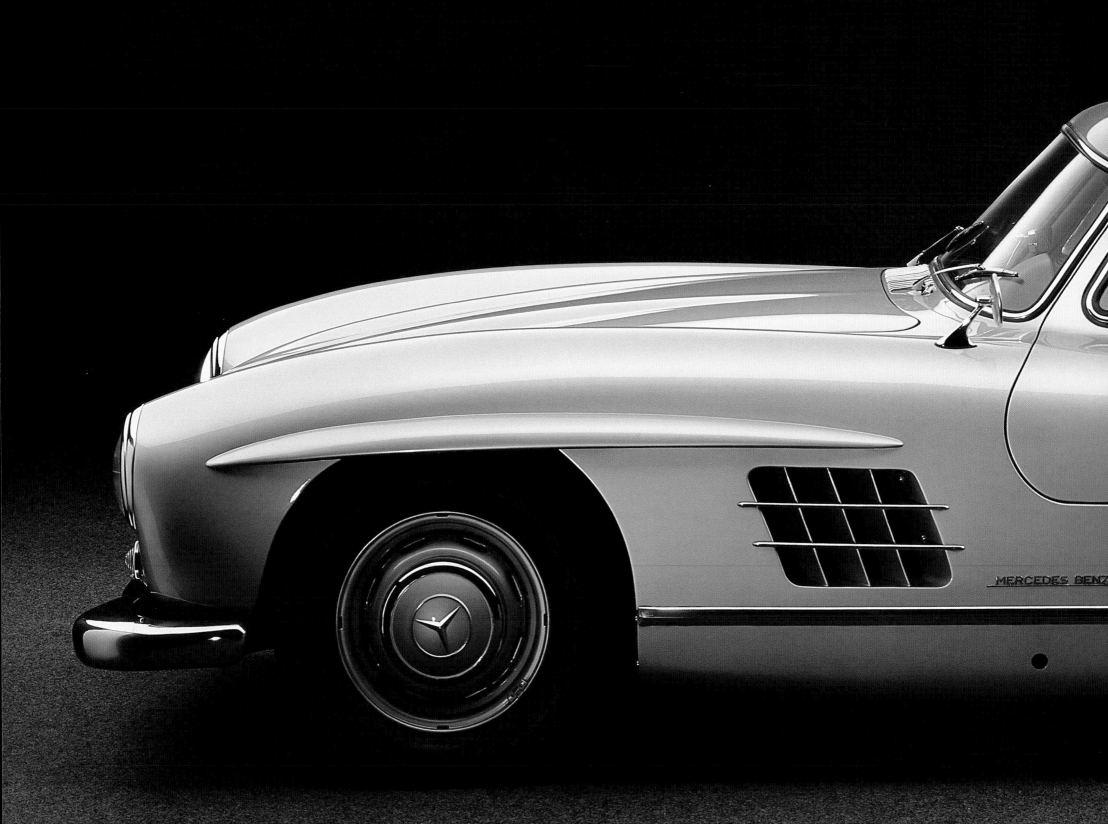

1955 FORD THUNDERBIRD

The original Ford Thunderbird was created as a reaction to the Chevrolet Corvette, and, as with the Corvette, its designers copied the main dimensions from the Jaguar XK120. Only the width differed, since it was necessary to use production axles. Franklin Hershey, the man who had put fins on the Cadillac in 1948, was the principal designer, and he very cleverly used a great deal of the mainstream 1955 Ford saloon body hardware, including front and rear lights and their surrounds.

The Corvette was presented as a 'pure' sports car with clip-on side curtains instead of roll-up windows, but there was no such intention at Ford. The Thunderbird was meant to be a 'personal car', not a sports cars, and it fell into the category of "gentleman's speedy roadster", this evocative phrase being taken from the model name of an American Stanley Steamer of 1904. The car was far more comfortable than the Corvette, and with a bigger V8 engine it was just about as fast in a straight line. There was a considerable difference in cornering ability, to the Corvette's advantage, but customers cared not a whit about that.

The scoop on the bonnet was a dummy, but the design was brilliant; it suited the times and the American clientele.

The Thunderbird was all steel, not the suspicious newfangled fibreglass of the Corvette body, and came with all the features available on standard Ford passenger cars. It was an immediate success, selling in the thousands while in the same year Corvettes sold in the hundreds .

Not suited to road racing, the Thunderbird was successful in straight-line speed trials, particularly when fitted with superchargers, yet the 'personal car' label was quite accurate and satisfied a wide range of buyers. The pink car seen here, built in 1956, was the property of Marilyn Monroe, who chose the popular 'continental kit' with outside spare wheel and tyre mounting. Chromed headlight bezels are non-standard, but the car otherwise represents a real piece of period Americana.

1955 PACKARD CARIBBEAN

This Caribbean convertible, first owned by the renowned French popular singer Edith Piaf, must have cut a dash in Paris with its multi-coloured paint scheme and flashy chrome trim. It was, in truth, a behemoth, and with its big engine it was quite quick in both acceleration and top speed, although its braking system, as was true for many cars at the time, hardly sufficed for sustained high-speed running. But, with its advanced torsion-bar suspension system linking front and rear wheels, it offered unequalled ride comfort, at least until the Citroën DS was introduced a year later. One can imagine that the diminutive stature of its original owner made the Caribbean seem bigger still, a larger-than-life car.

Even in its death throes, Packard was able to create impressive cars. There are many reasons why this pre-eminent American quality car company failed, but one must be the fact that, at the insistence of President Franklin D. Roosevelt, it sent its tooling for the Senior series cars to the Soviet Union as a perk for Stalin. When the war was over, only middle-range cars were available for sale, a real handicap. For 1948 a fat pontoon skin was laid over the 1941 Clipper, creating the unfortunate 'pregnant Packard'. The first true post-World War II Packard body did not appear until 1951, and an overhead-valve V8 engine arrived only for the 1955 models. Packard then bought Studebaker and the last real Packards were the 1956 models; after that rebadged Studebakers carried, and tarnished, the name.

Wartime profits from manufacturing aircraft and marine engines, in particular the Rolls-Royce Merlin V12, should have enabled Packard to prosper, but poor management decisions assured the demise of a company that had once enjoyed the highest reputation for quality and engineering prowess.

A gaudy giant, the Caribbean backed up its imposing presence with real performance from its new V8 engine.

Multiple colours bounded by chrome bands made for a look perfectly suited to an entertainer, but perhaps not to traditional Packard clients.

opposite
This aspect of the Caribbean was familiar to generations of Muscovites, who saw nearly identical Zil grilles on official limousines for decades after Packard died.

1955 CITROËN DS19

What one must understand about this car is that, however handsome it may be, its true value lies entirely beneath its multi-material skins (alloy bonnet and doors, steel wings, fibreglass roof). The styling simply consists of 1953 Studebaker coupé lines superimposed on the architecture of the 1934 Citroën 11. The engine, too, is that of the 1930s car. That may sound disturbingly derivative, but in fact this is the most technically advanced car, as compared to its contemporaries, ever put into production – any time, anywhere. The DS (*déesse*, or goddess, when the two letters are pronounced in French) had self-levelling suspension that used hydraulic fluid to compress nitrogen-filled bags inside steel spheres; an automatic clutch; and a pressure-sensitive 'mushroom' button on the floor to activate incredibly powerful inboard front-disk brakes. The delicate lever that started the engine also changed gears hydraulically. Like most of today's family cars, it had front-wheel-drive, but at a time when only a few obscure minor European makes featured it. Its interior was incredibly comfortable, with flow-through ventilation that obviated any need for vent windows. Thick layers of soft foam underlay the carpets, the seats used stretchy nylon jersey over more thick foam, and a wheelbase more than 3 metres (10 feet) long assured limousine-like room for rear passengers.

A single bolt held each wheel in place, and the car incorporated self-jacking. Side glass was frameless, A-pillars were slim, and the feel of being swept through space was – and still is today – exciting. Body detailing included inner door handles that demanded to be caressed and indicators on the C-pillars (added at the last minute because the translucent plastic roof panels on the first cars distorted, leaving a gap). The DS and its simplified sister, the ID (*idée*, or 'idea', in French, which featured a clutch pedal), were masterpieces of pure, brilliant design.

This ID19 from 1959 is a mechanically simplified version of the original DS19, visually identical apart from smaller hub caps and possessing the same astonishing level of comfort. The high indicator was a last-minute addition after the translucent roof panel had shrunk away from the C-pillar.

1956 LINCOLN CONTINENTAL MK II

Intended to be the highest-quality luxury car in the world, the Lincoln Continental Mk II was created under the direction of William Clay Ford, then twenty-six years old, who was the younger brother of Henry Ford II and father of current Ford Chairman Bill Ford. The project started in 1952 and had an on–off existence that culminated in the car that went on sale in autumn 1955.

Some of the best designers and engineers worked on the car. John Reinhart, formerly chief designer for Packard, headed the design team, and Gordon Buehrig, creator of many classics, most especially Duesenberg and Cord models, was the body engineer. Henry II disliked the first p.oposal, so W.C. Ford brought in four outside teams to provide alternatives. Nevertheless, the original internal team's new proposal won the contest, which was arranged so that each judge saw the projects alone, uninfluenced by hierarchy or family name.

The car was expensive, costing considerably more than a contemporary Rolls-Royce, and its mere existence galvanized General Motors, which authorized production of a Cadillac cost-no-object rival (the Eldorado Brougham). Every detail of the Continental was carefully thought out and every effort was made to ensure that each example was faultless. A telling detail was that each cross-head screw holding the inside windscreen moulding was aligned so that its slots were perfectly horizontal and vertical. The cars were constructed in a plant specially built for the purpose. To reduce the possibility of flaws, leather from Scotland, where barbed wire was not used, upholstered the cars, which were then shipped to dealers in fleece-lined covers. Most of the Continental Mk IIs made during its three-year run are in the hands of collectors today, but they have yet to make much impression in Concours d'Elégance, possibly because they are considered too recent to be classics.

The wire wheels of the Lincoln were simply very expensive covers for ordinary pressed-steel units.

left
The spare wheel cover was seen as a trademark feature of the Continental. It persisted right through to the Mk VIII version, usually without a tyre inside.

opposite
Although it was handsome enough, the Mk II lacked the panache that had made Edsel Ford's personal 1939 Continental, and those produced from 1940 to 1948, so special.

1957 LOTUS ELITE

Although commercially disastrous, the Lotus Elite GT coupé was a technical tour de force when it was first presented during the 1957 London Motor Show at Earl's Court. The concept was to make a unit-construction body-chassis unit entirely of fibreglass-reinforced polyester resin, the thin skins being the primary structure. The materials and techniques had been in use for a decade or more for boats, and for certain non-load-bearing body parts, such as the outer skins of the Chevrolet Corvette of 1953. Unfortunately, the design methods used were far more appropriate for metal than for plastics, and more than a few severe accidents occurred in endurance races when the inboard rear brake discs heated and softened the material, causing it to fail catastrophically.

The original Elite was a model of simple elegance with beautiful surfaces and understated detail design. This model is from 1965.

But the car was a brilliantly conceived product for normal road use, its intended primary purpose. The engine was an ultra-lightweight Coventry-Climax unit, originally designed for a firefighter's pump and meant to be hand-carried by two men. When adapted to automotive use, it allowed for very high performance in terms of both speed and economy; this was due to the fact that the car weighed so little – 488 kg (1076 lb) without fuel, according to most sources. Only 988 units were made, in three separate series, during its six-year life. The elegant and advanced shape was created by Peter Kirwan-Taylor, a financial expert from the City of London, who not only gave the coupé its form, but also arranged the finance that allowed it to be produced.

Because Lotus founder Colin Chapman had made his automotive reputation with racing cars, and because the Elite was so obviously suited for racing, it was immediately adopted for competition, winning the first time it was raced and going on to win the 1500 cc class at the 24 Hours at Le Mans in 1959, despite having an engine of only 1216 cc. It finished eighth overall, an outstanding accomplishment.

Aerodynamically and aesthetically correct, the Elite was a masterpiece. It was shaped not by a stylist, but by a financial man from the City of London, Peter Kirwan-Taylor.

The tiny Elite has a
disproportionately large top,
yet it works visually because
of the balance of the whole.

1959 AUSTIN SE7EN (MORRIS MINI MINOR)

The fusion of those great rivals Austin and Morris in 1952 gave rise to little of note. The Austin A-40 engine replaced the antique side-valve unit in the Morris Minor, and here and there a little component-sharing took place. But when the Suez crisis of 1956 made fuel economy all-important, Alec Issigonis, a Morris engineer, was ready with a new concept: a car only 3 metres (10 feet) long, in which 80% of the length was given over to four passengers and the other 20% sufficed for mechanicals and luggage. This was accomplished by turning the engine sideways and putting the gearbox in its sump – a bad, if imaginative, idea.

Apart from their badges, the Austin and Morris models were identical, but the quaint alphanumeric spelling 'Se7en' never caught on, and to the whole world the little motorized brick shape was 'the Mini'. The cars were horrid in some respects: the body flanges turned inward, ensuring that water would leak in and have no way to exit, and the ignition distributor was placed so that rain coming in from the front would short it. Issigonis had the absurd idea that an uncomfortable driver would be more alert, so on safety grounds he specified a contorted driving position.

No matter. The car handled better than most racing cars and was immediately adopted by all social classes as their own, making the Mini classless – a revolutionary idea in the stratified England of the 1950s and one perfectly suited to the Swinging Sixties. *Autocar* said that the Issigonis Mini was never profitable in its four decades of production, but it influenced manufacturers everywhere, all of whom did a better job of engineering, though not of imagination. If the Fiat 128 is the true prototype of the modern family car, the Mini was its inspiration.

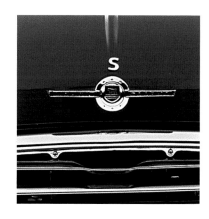

The little brick-shaped Mini existed in many guises; this one is the 1965 Mini Cooper with enhanced performance and alloy wheels.

left
The near-antique long-stroke BMC
'A' engine was pushed up to 1275 cc.
This, combined with the Mini's
superb handling, made the car a
giant-beater in races and rallies.

opposite
Mini-creator Alec Issigonis thought
that an uncomfortable driver was a
safer one (less likely to fall asleep).
So he made the Mini very safe,
giving it a terrible driving position.

1960 CHEVROLET CORVAIR

The rear-engine Chevrolet Corvair was one of the so-called 'compact' cars created by Detroit in reaction to the rising success of small imported cars, chiefly the VW Type 1 'Beetle'. It was by any standards a poor car, with dangerous handling characteristics, an engine that leaked oil fumes into the ventilation system, and shamefully poor crashworthiness. Social critic Ralph Nader, who ran for President against George W. Bush, had become a national figure over thirty years earlier as a result of his 1966 book *Unsafe at Any Speed*, which dealt with the Corvair's drastic shortcomings.

But the Corvair was superbly shaped and had enormous influence on subsequent cars throughout the world. Its perimeter line and thin roof were picked up in Germany by BMW for the 1502 and by NSU for the Prinz; in Italy, by Fiat for the 1300 and 1500 saloons; in France, by Panhard for its 24-series cars, Simca for the 1000 and Renault for its R8; in Japan, by Hino for the Contessa and Mazda for the 800; in England, by Hillman for the Imp; and even by Zaporozhets in the Soviet Union – an astonishing achievement.

Under the direction of William Mitchell, who succeeded Harley J. Earl as Vice President of Design at General Motors, the principal stylist was Ned Nickles, whose work at GM was often outstanding. This Corvair, the 1951 Le Sabre concept car and the 1963 Buick Riviera all came from his drawing board.

Japanese-American 'Bud' Sugano invented the 'flying wing' roof, which turned out to be so wonderfully adaptable to small European and Japanese cars but was also successfully used for huge GM saloons in 1959–60. Unusually for an American design, there were no artifices, no imitation grille in front, no extraneous non-functional trim. A handsome station wagon was built on the same platform. A coupé was less attractive with its more conventional roof, but the convertible is considered collectible today.

This 1962 version of the Corvair had a convex area between the headlights that carried ignominious imitation air intakes. The purity of line remained intact, however.

The interior of the Corvair was austere for an American car. It was meant to be a rival to the Volkswagen 'Beetle', after all.

opposite
For all its simplicity of shape, there was plenty of brightwork on the Corvair.

The air-cooled engine's horizontal fan was driven by a vee-belt running at right angles over pulleys.

1960 VOLVO P-1800

Volvo played with the idea of sports cars for a while before finally committing to serious production of this coupé. A small series of Dutch Darrin-designed 1900 roadsters with fibreglass bodies convinced the Swedish firm that there was a market for a car that was not purely functional transport. The shape of the P-1800 was essentially inspired by a series of Carrozzeria Ghia 'Supersonic' models on various chassis, although the derivative Volvo design was drawn up in Sweden. Body production was at first carried out in England by Jensen Motors, but quality was not up to Volvo's standards, and as the sports coupé was the most expensive model in the line, the car was damaging the company's reputation.

So, for 1963, tooling was moved to Sweden and the cars were built entirely in-house. To make the change known, P-1800 S (for Sweden) became the new model name. The car was a little heavy for its 1800 cc engine, but it was solid and well behaved on the road. Volvo rejected an American project to fit 4.7-litre Ford engines despite highly satisfactory test results because, said Volvo's chairman Gunnar Engellau, "People will think there is something wrong with our motor." Evolution of the basic design into a sports wagon and engine growth to 2 litres helped, but the 1800 ES was never a performance car in the accepted sense.

What the P-1800 S demonstrated is that high style combined with solid – even stolid – reliability was a winning formula, one that Japanese companies recognized and exploited with great success. Strangely, Volvo itself did not understand what it had achieved, and moved away from overtly sporting looks to fairly restrained saloon-like coupés from Bertone and then built its own coupés and convertibles in the C-70 models. None sold as well as the bold and imaginative 1800s.

Inspired by a 1952 Italian design, the P-1800 was introduced in 1960 and remained in production more than ten years, first as a coupé and later as a sports wagon. This example is a P-1800 E from 1970.

1961 JAGUAR E-TYPE

Company boss Sir William Lyons designed most Jaguar bodies himself, including the SS90 and SS100 two-seat sports cars before World War II and the XK120 roadster immediately afterwards. He was, however, more of a saloon-car specialist than a sports-car designer (the XK120 had been copied from a Carrozzeria Touring body on a BMW) so he left much of the design of the E-Type to Malcolm Sayer, the aerodynamicist who had shaped the brilliant XK-D sports racers that won Le Mans three times in 1955–57. Sayer had created an oval-section central body – directly inspired by Touring's Disco Volante designs for Alfa Romeo – that was constructed very much like an aeroplane fuselage in light alloy, then he appended a tubular-steel truss to the firewall to carry the engine and front suspension. The fuel tank and rear axle hung off the back of the monocoque, which was covered by unstressed light-alloy body panels. The D was exotic, but it was practical; Jaguar mechanics drove the cars from Brown's Lane, Coventry, to the circuit at Le Mans.

When the E-Type was unveiled at the Geneva Motor Show in 1961, it astonished the world. Not only did it continue the D-Type's aeronautical central structure (but in steel this time), but it actually had far more advanced suspension (independent on all four wheels), better roadholding, and a top speed of 241 kph (150 mph). It was offered in both roadster and fastback coupé forms. Its performance equalled that of the best cars of the time, but it cost far less than contemporary Ferrari and Mercedes two-seaters. Launched with the 3.8-litre version of the venerable XK twin-cam six-cylinder engine, it gained more displacement three years later with a 4.2-litre powerplant. There were three series of E-Types, the last also available with the powerful but thirsty Jaguar V12 engine.

The automotive sex symbol of the 1960s, the E-Type dazzled the public with its astonishing performance and relatively low price.

Even with the cloth top in place,
the elegance of the E-Type was
not compromised in the least. It is
spectacularly beautiful.

The voluptuous sensuality of the front was maintained perfectly in the upswept tail panel with dual exhausts beneath.

The virtually flawless composition of the front end of the E-Type evoked admiration everywhere and recalled the Le Mans-winning D-Type racers.

1961 ASTON MARTIN DB4 GT ZAGATO

If, at times, it seems that there have been as many Aston Martin company owners as there have been cars carrying the revered name, for the past decade and a half there has been stability, with the Ford Motor Company doing a splendid job of stewardship of the legend. From its inception in 1914 until Ford acquired it in 1987, Aston Martin had many successes and even more setbacks. The threads running through Aston Martin history were strength, quality and a commitment to competition. Founder Lionel Martin did well at the Aston Clinton hillclimb in Buckinghamshire in 1914, and appended the name of the venue to his own. Subsequent company owners also relied on competition success to surmount financial difficulties.

There was always a strong Italian connection, too. Augustus Cesare Bertelli took over from Martin, and the 'Bertelli Astons' became successful racers, winning the Biennial Cup at Le Mans in 1932 with Bertelli himself in the driving seat. Industrialist David Brown bought the company in 1947, and by the mid-1950s he had turned to Italy for body designs: Carrozzeria Touring for the 1968 DB4 and DB4 GT, and Zagato for a competition model on the GT chassis. Using a tuned version of the in-house 3.7-litre six-cylinder engine designed by Tadek Marek, only nineteen of these 314 hp Zagato cars were built over a three-year period (1961–63). Although world champion Jimmy Clark and Le Mans winner Roy Salvadori raced them, they never quite had the measure of the Ferrari GTO. The sheer beauty of the aerodynamic Zagato bodywork created by Zagato's young styling director Ercole Spada, along with their rarity, makes these Astons prized collector's items. Fortunately, many are still used in historic racing, so there are still opportunities to see them in action.

The voluptuous curves of the Zagato Aston Martin allow no doubt as to the purpose of this rare competition model. The oversized grille helps cool the highly tuned engine and lends the car an aggressive appearance.

1962 FERRARI 250 GTO

In the 1960s, to qualify for the Grand Touring racing category, the FIA (Fédération Internationale de l'Automobile) required that a manufacturer should produce fifty identical examples of a specific model. Ferrari certified that it had met the requirements and even named its racing GT car 250 GTO (Gran Turismo Omologato) to emphasize the point. One of the greatest of all Ferraris, the GTO was in fact completely fraudulent, with only thirty-seven chassis built by the factory, each with considerable variation in body shape and detail. Nevertheless, it was a magnificent machine, so highly prized that the example used by Jean Guichet to win the European GT championship in 1964 was purchased by a Japanese collector for $15 million in the late 1980s.

Falsification continues to this day, with numerous 'GTOs' having been constructed using more mundane 250 GT components. As with many classic cars, more examples exist now than the factory built, but only the thirty-seven original chassis plates are real, and as GTO owner Nick Mason, who races his hard in vintage events, says, "That [chassis indentification] plate is what's valuable." Anything else can be rebuilt, so he does not treat his car as a delicate showpiece.

Whether true or false, driven hard or kept in a museum, GTOs are absolutely magnificent, with unequalled proportions for the volumes of the bodywork and an elegant austerity in the shaping of such details as the hot-air outlets on the front wings and the transparent fairings over the headlights. There is no décor, no extraneous trim, yet even the interiors are shaped with that typical Italian concern for beauty. Not for these Ferrari masterpieces the technical fighter-plane instrumentation often seen on racing cars from other countries. Italian coachbuilders just naturally mount the gauges in gently curved sections of the fascia, always seeking elegance.

The Ferrari prancing horse is drawn from the coat of arms of the city of Stuttgart. The two leading sports-car manufacturers of the twenty-first century share the same emblem.

opposite

Italians can't help themselves. The panel may be as functional as that of a fighter aeroplane, but the steering wheel, the gear stick and the composition are beautiful.

right and below right

Proof that this is a racer: the small air inlet that relies upon speed to ensure adequate flow through the radiator. The rear is truncated according to the theories of the famed German aerodynamicist Dr Wunibald Kamm.

1963 PORSCHE 911

One of the longest-lived designs in automotive history, the Porsche 911 has been produced for forty years, evolving from a 2-litre coupé with 150 hp running on narrow 165-15 tyres to 3.6-litre turbocharged machines capable of supercar performance, along the way giving birth to the 935 variants that won the Le Mans 24 Hours outright. The basic lines of the 911, drawn by Ferdinand 'Butzi' Porsche in the mid-1950s, were faithfully preserved through several chassis iterations. The car shown here, labelled 912, is the most basic of the whole series, equipped with a four-cylinder engine as a cost-cutting measure; it is, however, externally identical to the Frankfurt show car of 1963.

Often cited as 'a triumph of development over bad design', the Porsche 911 is magnificent today, but in the beginning it was so disappointing that Porsche fired Dr Tomala, chief engineer on the project. Over the years the engine was moved forward, the wheelbase was increased, the basic suspension system was revised several times, four-wheel drive was added for some models and width increased, yet the basic lines, particularly the side-window profile, have persisted unchanged.

Erwin Kommenda, Professor Porsche's body designer, laid out the shape of the 356 model, basing it on a VW racing coupé created in 1939, and Butzi Porsche developed that into the longer, less podgy form of the 911. Subsequent Porsche chief designers Anatole Lapine and Harm Lagaay polished and refined the basics, taking into account newly acquired information about aerodynamics and allowing for wider – much wider – wheels and tyres.

Part of the charm of the car is its relatively small size: the cosy cockpit and the visual allure of the rounded front wings as seen from the driver's seat. Slated for oblivion more than twenty years ago, the 911 shape will continue into the foreseeable future.

Forty years on, this is one of the most familiar sports-car shapes in the world. This 1967 model is almost unchanged from the car first shown at Frankfurt in 1963.

The roof and windscreen profiles have endured for the entire life of the 911, and the variant introduced in 2004 continued the classic form.

1965 TOYOTA 2000 GT

Toyota's 2000 GT was seen as 'the Japanese E-Type', its proportions closely matching those of Jaguar's classic British coupé, but its design was derived from a prototype that was to become the Datsun 240Z at the beginning of the 1970s. When German-American Count Albrecht Goertz created his early design for the Datsun, he did so in the workshops of the Yamaha company, known in the motoring world for its motorcycles. These workshops were in fact related to the company's manufacture of musical instruments, among them excellent pianos. Pianos used wires to make sound; motorcycles used them in their wheels. Wind instruments use pressure waves in shaped tubes to make sounds, and pressure waves in tubes make for good cylinder-filling in engines. All very logical to the Japanese, apparently.

Yamaha designed the twin-cam cylinder head of the 2000 GT and applied it to a Toyota truck-engine block. The much smaller six-cylinder engine looked very much like the E-Type's. One sees in some of the body details, specifically the small service flaps alongside the bonnet in both the Toyota and the Datsun, that Goertz's work informed both cars, although he did not execute the production form of either. Only a few hundred 2000 GTs were made, including a couple of convertibles used in a James Bond film. Some were left-hand drive for the USA and continental Europe, but the price was far too high – higher than the bigger and faster Jaguar, for example – for the jewel-like car to have ever been a big seller. Also, interior space was severely limited, with anyone of above-average height suffering some discomfort as his or her head touched the roof. Despite this, the 2000 GT, built on its own chassis of quite advanced design for the time, is a true thoroughbred.

above
The aerodynamic wing mirror, popular in the 1960s, clearly betrays the age of the 2000 GT.

opposite
The overall design of the 2000 GT was influenced by the British Lotus Elan (for the chassis) and the E-Type Jaguar (its proportions), as well as the Datsun 240Z, which was prototyped in the same Yamaha workshops.

Body hardware was beautifully
made – probably by hand, given
the limited volume. Just 337 units
were produced, of which two were
convertibles made for a James
Bond film.

The twin-cam engine was
converted from a basic Toyota
unit by Yamaha and built to a
high standard of finish.

opposite
The cockpit, inspired by Lotus,
was made with exceptional care –
especially the central console.
The fit was flawless.

1972 BMW TURBO CONCEPT COUPÉ

In some respects this striking, mid-engine GT car is an elaborate inside joke. Paul Bracq, the French chief designer for BMW, and Bob Lutz, the Swiss–American marketing manager, desperately wanted to produce a sports car, but BMW's management was willing only to fund a research project for a 'safety car', a sober manifesto that showed the seriousness of the company. Somehow the two executives managed to persuade their colleagues that their car was just such an object. Upper management asked them to paint the car grey to emphasize its sobriety, but the cheerful conspirators explained that fluorescent ends in International Orange were justified so that it would be visible to pedestrians in foggy or rainy conditions – an irrefutable safety argument.

It might have been an outrageous safety car, but it was the perfect expression of what BMW was becoming: a company orientated towards driving pleasure and performance. After years of Isetta single-cylinder bubble cars, saloons and coupés powered by BMW's flat-twin motorcycle engine, and other austerity products suited to the rebuilding of Germany, turbocharged road rockets were exactly what the customers wanted to see, and the Turbo was a sensation at motor shows all over the world. Although production was never authorized, the Turbo did eventually lead to the limited-production M-1 coupé, a bigger, more powerful but less attractive design carried out in collaboration with ItalDesign in Turin.

Through this and other high-powered models based on production saloons and coupés, BMW made itself the iconic car for the 'Baby Boomer' generation in America and for ambitious young entrepreneurs in Swinging London. It is no accident that car advertising all over the world presents new products aimed at the upper reaches of the middle class as "like a BMW". The Turbo had a huge part in creating the BMW legend.

A 'safety car' conceit was used to justify the fluorescent-orange end panels of this extremely dramatic show car.

left
This cockpit, with its instruments angled towards the driver, was very much inspired by racing GT cars and in turn influenced later BMW production models.

opposite
Gull-wing doors were necessary for same reason that they were used in 1950s Mercedes racers: to allow access across broad sills.

1975 VOLKSWAGEN GOLF

At the end of the 1960s Volkswagenwerk AG was a dying company. It had little to sell beyond the air-cooled, rear-engine designs derived from the 'Strength through Joy' Beetle, or 'Bug', of the 1930s, itself fading as a product. VW was saved by two brilliant Italians, Dante Giacosa and Giorgietto Giugiaro.

Giacosa, an engineer who spent his entire career with Fiat, invented the mechanical layout used by most of the world's cars today, in which a gearbox is driven directly off the crankshaft of an engine mounted transversely in the nose of the car. This was cribbed by VW engineers for the Golf. Giugiaro, the most prolific designer of the modern era, says that the best and most important design he has ever done was this first Golf. In 1969 Kurt Lotz was head of VW, and he knew he needed new styling. He noted the six cars he liked best at the Turin Motor Show that year, and when he discovered that four were by Giugiaro he hired the stylist's ItalDesign for his new model programme.

The first car to be produced, in 1973, was the Passat, which had a traditional, longitudinally mounted engine but front-wheel drive. Then a new man, Rudolf Leiding, took over at VW and immediately cancelled all the Giugiaro cars except the Golf, stating, "It can't work, but it's too late to change it." Leiding's luck was much better than his judgement, because the Golf was a best-seller from its introduction in 1975, and continues today in its fifth generation. There was never a clearer indication of the power of good design. The Golf's key elements – a simple rectangular air intake flanked by round headlights at the corners, simplified body panels with shallow draw depth for the stamping presses and stiffening ribs to assure a solid structure, along with the car's crisp linearity – established a look that was widely copied.

The Golf GTi was the performance model of the VW Golf line, inspiring every manufacturer in Europe to make a 'hot hatch'. This 1983 Trophy model was the last of the series 1 Golfs.

Something this simple and direct might seem easy to achieve. It is not: it takes design genius and accurate manufacture.

From the rear the Golf is really just a little box, but the crisp delineation of lights, hatch and bumper shows Giugiaro's design mastery to great advantage.

opposite

The Giugiaro 'folded paper' style worked better on exterior surfaces than inside the car. The entire interior seems, and is, dated and uninteresting by modern standards. It was, however, much loved and much imitated in the later 1970s.

1987 PORSCHE 959

Conceived as a competition car but never used as such, the 959 was a technological masterpiece that appeared just a little too late for its intended purpose. This car and several contemporary rivals were called 'the Killer Bees', a series of extraordinary high-performance road cars created primarily for international rallying. The sobriquet came from the fact that the no-holds-barred category under which such cars – made in at least 200 identical examples – were homologated was officially designated Group B. In fact, Group B cars were much too fast, and after a fatal accident in the Rally of Corsica in 1986 they were banned from competition. Ferrari had already built its second GTO and Peugeot its 205 Turbo 16 when the ban was instituted, but Porsche was in the midst of development of the 959.

The company decided to carry on and made 250 units, some of them fully trimmed with all comfort items, including automatic air conditioning, others stripped out for lighter weight and even higher performance, as though 322 kph (200 mph) were not enough. The cars were snapped up by collectors for some £150,000 each – among whom was the richest man in the world, Bill Gates, although 959s were not legal in the USA – and all but disappeared from public view. With electronically controlled four-wheel drive, and electronically managed sequential turbocharging to assure massive power and torque no matter what the engine speed, 959s were paragons of flexibility and usability. However, because attainment of the car's incredibly high speeds was so simple, requiring no special driving skills, several press people remarked that while it was all very impressive, it was not much fun.

Although the 959 looks much like production 911s, only the side glass is common. All panels are differently shaped and of different materials from those used in normal all-steel Porsches.

Viewed in profile, it is easy to see that the central portion of the normal 911 body shape was retained for this cost-no-object supercar. The wheels look too close together because of added front and rear overhang.

Appendages to the body include a longer nose, a wider track with enveloping mudguards, and the rear wing, all needed for stability at 320 kph (200 mph).

below right

(Barely) recognizable as a Porsche 911, the 959 is a striking object with its many scoops, holes and vents.

opposite

Tucking the standard tail shape into a huge wing assures that lift will be overcome and that substantial downforce will be applied to the body as speed rises. It is a very dramatic look.

1988   FERRARI F40

It has become a tradition for Ferrari to offer a road car with racing-car performance – but not true racing capability – every decade or so. These art-object cars have always been exciting-looking, apparently intended for competition, but in fact they are intended to act as a magnet for collectors, and as a reliable profit centre for Ferrari – a way to defray some of the development costs for the less exotic production models. The first of these not-quite racing cars was the 288 GTO of 1984, a higher-performance version of the popular 'Magnum' 308 GT. A total of 272 were made and sold at quite high prices, and many were then quickly resold by the first owners at more than 100% profit.

The lesson was not lost on Ferrari, which issued the F40 four years later, at a much higher price; and in great quantity, with 1311 units sold. Built to commemorate the fortieth anniversary of Enzo Ferrari's eponymous car company, the turbocharged F40 was one of the first true 'art cars', in the sense that it was built neither to a racing brief, nor to provide comfortable, luxurious individualized transport for connoisseurs, but simply to be an object of desire. One could suggest that the F40 was a cynical exercise in profit-making, rather like a Hummel figurine, meant only to be collected by those with surplus funds.

This is not to say that the F40 was not a wonderful vehicle, well developed and capable of very high levels of performance on a weekend drive. But it was equipped summarily and was not truly luxurious or even sufficiently comfortable to be an acceptable grand tourer. The F40's desirability is inextricably linked to the mythos of the Ferrari name, and to the firm's purity of purpose in building only cars with a racing heritage. And it is brutally beautiful and exciting.

above
The flush, low-drag NACA duct for cabin ventilation and the lamps covered by flaps during the daytime are designed to convey the impression of speed and advanced technology.

opposite
The F40 in all its imitation race-car regalia. Every detail is designed to be functional, but in a marketing rather than a technical sense.

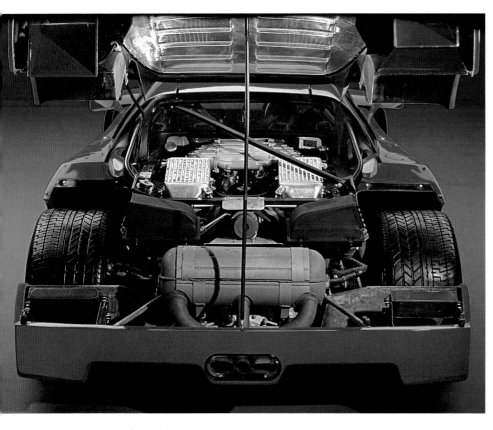

Under the tail panel there is plenty
of visual entertainment for owners
to show their friends.

With the tail panel closed, there
is still much surface decoration
and presumed technology on
show. The high wing is particularly
impressive, as is the ventilated
plastic rear windscreen.

Who would not feel like a hero
approaching this no-nonsense,
all-business object with keys
in hand?

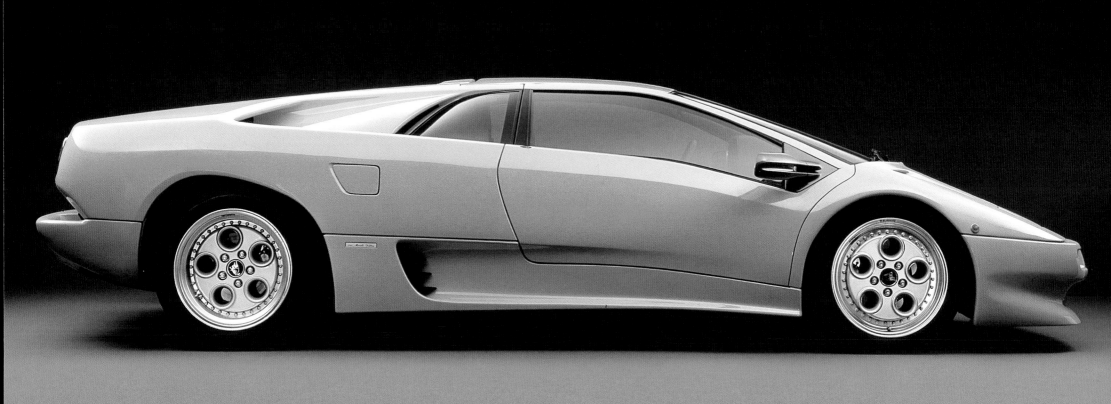

1990 LAMBORGHINI DIABLO

No modern automotive firm has had as chequered a history as the sports-car company founded by Ferruccio Lamborghini. Legend has it that Lamborghini, disgusted at having been made to wait for hours to talk with Enzo Ferrari about problems he was having with his car, stormed out of the factory vowing to make his own cars. As a successful tractor manufacturer, he was in a position, financially and technically, to do just that, and he did so with a vengeance – quite literally. His first model, the 350GT (shown in 1963), had a V12 engine with a body by Carrozzeria Touring, but Lamborghini shifted his allegiance to Giuseppe 'Nuccio' Bertone and a series of spectacular models followed, including the 'impossible' Miura with its V12 engine transversely mounted behind the seats, giving Lamborghini a huge lead over Ferrari. But Lamborghini eventually grew tired of the expense and frustrations inherent in making cars in small quantities. (For Enzo Ferrari these psychological burdens were compensated for by the pleasures of racing. Indeed, Ferrari cared only for competition on the track and could easily ignore the other side of his business.)

Various groups have owned Lamborghini since then, including Chrysler. The Diablo was created under Chrysler's ownership and its styling is a mix of Italian and American ideas, all the more unusual in that Lamborghini now belongs to Volkswagen's Audi division. The overblown, dramatic looks of the Diablo contrast mightily with the more austere Germanic styling of the latest Lamborghinis. That the firm is now soundly based and that its engineering is more methodical (if less exciting) are all to the good, but the Diablo will remain for ever the last Lamborghini made in the old, Italian spirit.

The Diablo is far too powerful for most drivers to be able to control with only rear-wheel drive, so four-wheel drive has been made standard, consistent with Audi's policy for all its performance models.

The dramatic Diablo profile owes a great deal to Marcello Gandini, designer of some of Bertone's best Lamborghinis, but it has been tweaked by many other designers and is a less than pure expression of form.

Conducting heat away from the engine compartment is a constant challenge for designers. Scoops on the body side carry air through the compartment to be flushed through vents on top and at the rear.

opposite
Very fast cars must always have lamps available for instant flashing, here tucked below the bumper strike face. The doors pivot forwards to simplify entry.

266

1995 FERRARI F50 PININFARINA

If the F40 was purely a commercial proposition based on series production components, the F50 was a truly ambitious technical exercise incorporating a tremendous amount of hard-earned Formula One racing technology. It was, in a sense, a two-seat version of Ferrari single-seaters, its V12 engine enlarged to 4.7 litres, using steel valve springs rather than the pneumatic closure mechanism of the racers. A direct and basic car, it lacked power-assisted steering or braking, although air conditioning was standard equipment.

While the F40 was turbocharged, the F50's engine is an atmospheric unit that makes its 500-plus hp at 8500 rpm rather than 14,000. The body was styled by Pininfarina, using Ferrari's Formula One wind tunnel for verification. Perhaps the least beautiful of Ferrari's 'art cars', it nevertheless has undeniable presence and is considerably more authentic than its predecessors. The chassis is made entirely of carbon composite, whereas the F40 had carbon-fibre pieces attached to a tubular-steel structure. And, as in racing cars, the suspension was attached to the structure, with no bushings or other filters for vibration and noise. Despite this, the F50 is said to be perfectly tolerable on normal roads, although the sound of the mechanics has been described as almost overwhelming.

The cockpit is austere: there is upholstery on the seats and leather on the steering wheel, but apart from this all surfaces are left bare, with the raw material of construction showing. Not since the days of Bugattis in the 1920s and 1930s has a road car been as closely related to a top-line racing car. The F50 was truly a Formula One car for the road, and if only 349 were made, that is still a greater number of cars than there are drivers fully capable of exploiting the performance on offer.

Functional sculpture: Pininfarina took great care to make openings elegant as well as effective.

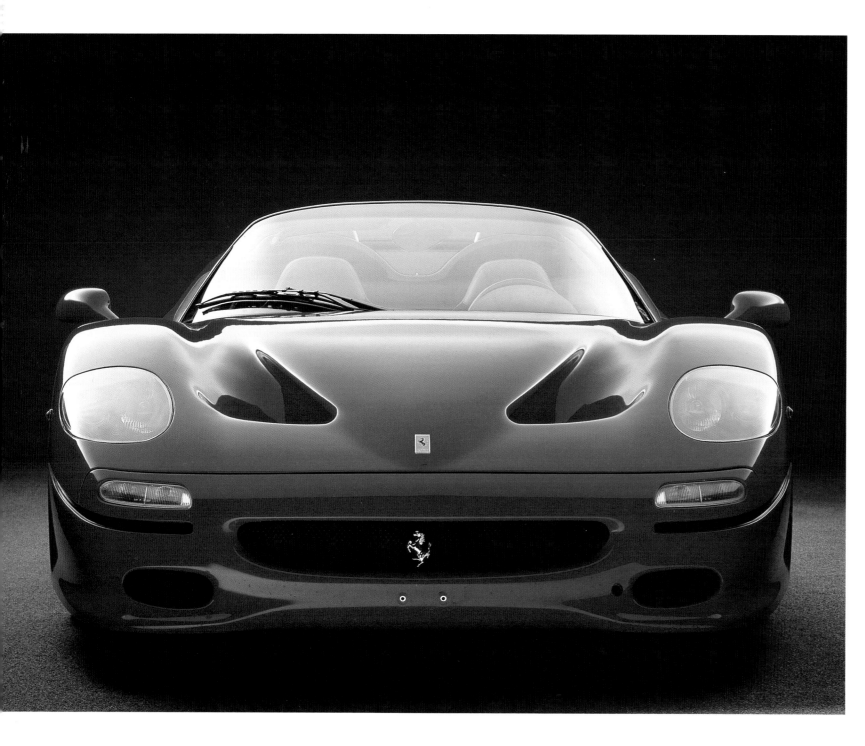

left
Perhaps the most harmonious view of the F50, in which ones sees the efforts of Pininfarina stylists to soften and add elegance to necessary ducts and spoilers.

opposite
The Formula One influence can easily be seen in the complex venting and ducting, and in the provision of serious roll-over protection that rises above the twin headrests.

2002 FERRARI ENZO FERRARI
PININFARINA

The ultimate art-object car is the Ferrari Enzo Ferrari, a model named to honour the company's founder and incorporating all of the technology of Ferrari's Formula One racing car. And, for once, there is true racing capability that will be demonstrated in public, although not directly under the Ferrari banner. Fiat, parent company of both Ferrari and Maserati, has decreed that Ferrari will continue to contest Formula One, in which it won five consecutive world championships in 1999–2003, and that in future Maserati will be the standard-bearer for sports-car racing, including the most important event of all, the Le Mans 24 Hours. To the delight of Ferrari enthusiasts, the new Maserati sports racer is based on the Enzo Ferrari chassis, with slightly different bodywork but all Formula One technology intact.

To be allowed to acquire an Enzo Ferrari, one must be a known long-time Ferrari client. Even with a $600,000-plus price tag, the 349 cars scheduled to be made – one fewer than the projected market, to ensure exclusivity – were snapped up in short order, leaving some valued customers in the cold. Luca di Montezemolo, the aristocratic leader of the firm, relented and added fifty cars to the build list, but even before the whole run has been made cars are changing hands at double the list price – an indication of the fervent desire of collectors to have the latest and greatest iconic car.

Di Montezemolo insisted that there be no wings, flaps or fins on the Enzo Ferrari, and the designers and engineers were so successful in reducing both drag and lift that it was necessary to detune the engine to prevent the top speed exceeding the ability of tyres to survive; not that there are many places where more than 400 kph (249 mph) can be sustained.

Looking a little like a helmet from *Star Wars*, the front of the Enzo Ferrari is far more technical than beautiful. It is, however, a highly impressive piece of work with unimaginable (and essentially unusable) performance, thanks to a large-displacement version of a Formula One engine.

above

The steering wheel contains multiple controls, as on a Formula One car, but also incorporates an airbag.

left

The heart of all Ferrari automobiles is the engine, and here is a unit at once beautiful and highly effective. It had to be detuned to keep speeds in line with tyre capability.

opposite

Not exactly an object of beauty, but neither is it a brutal expression of technical prowess. There is no rear wing, a requirement of Ferrari chairman Luca di Montezemolo that challenged Pininfarina designers to go beyond common knowledge. Truly a legend in the making.

The Enzo Ferrari profile is an artful combination of extreme grace and aggression, the perfect distillation of more than half a century of Ferrari sports cars. Tail lights are like rocket exhausts, a tip of Pininfarina's hat to American cars of the 1950s.

DESIGNER PROFILES

David Bache
British

Although he shaped many cars during his career, the late David Bache will forever be best known for a single design, his masterpiece: the 1970 Range Rover. Taking a simple, box-shaped prototype created by Rover's brilliant, absent-minded chief engineer, Spencer King, Bache modulated the form with radii here and there, and achieved an almost mystically perfect balance of volumes and proportions that established for all time the standard by which beauty in Sports Utility Vehicles (SUVs) would be judged.

The Range Rover has been restyled twice in thirty-three years, but the theme, the stance and the overall look remain as established by Bache. The Rover company changed hands three times during those years, first being absorbed by British Leyland, then sold to BMW and finally to Ford. In each instance the attraction was due to the status of the Range Rover as the pinnacle of an entire segment of the car industry.

Flaminio Bertoni
Italian-French

A true Renaissance man, Bertoni was first of all an artist, accomplished as both painter and sculptor. Born in Varese, Italy, in 1903, he went at the age of twenty to France, where in 1932 he was hired by André Citroën to shape the 'Traction Avant'. He created the immortal 2CV in the 1930s. Although no beauty, it was rigorously rational, with aerodynamic stability characteristics unaltered as the load in the car increased.

Always fascinated by architecture, Bertoni created a car-design centre – never built – that even today rivals in its vision the best studios of the richest car companies. He qualified for a degree in architecture in 1949, and won first prizes for drawings and sculpture at the International Free Art show in Paris in 1953, 1954, 1959 and 1962. He designed the radical Citroën DS19 in the early 1950s and the unlovely but logical Ami 6 before retiring. Bertoni died, much honoured, in 1964.

Carlo Felice Bianchi-Anderloni
Italian

When his father died in 1948, Carlo Felice Bianchi-Anderloni inherited Carrozzeria Touring. The consensus was that the Milan-based body builder would disappear because the young heir would not have the skill or experience to save the company. Two acts of masterful creation put an end to such talk. One was the *barchetta* ('little boat') body that Bianchi-Anderloni created for the first envelope-bodied Ferrari, the shape that won the 24 Hours at Le Mans in 1949 and that Touring continued to build for the next five years. The other was an Alfa Romeo coupé on the 6C 2500 SS chassis, which took first prize at Italy's Villa d'Este Concours d'Elégance in 1949.

Bianchi-Anderloni was the man behind the first bodies for Bristol and Lamborghini cars and the most spectacular ones for Pegasos. He created the Aston Martin DB4 and DB5 shapes, and finished his career with fifteen years as head of the body department at Alfa Romeo. He died in 2003.

Gordon Buehrig
American

At the age of twenty-five Gordon Buehrig became chief (and only) designer for Duesenberg. That was in 1929, just five months before the US stock market crash guaranteed the demise of the luxury marque. Over the next three years Buehrig designed almost half of all the Duesenberg J bodies actually built – a tremendous achievement. He had two brief stints with Harley Earl in General Motors' Art and Color staff before and after Duesenberg.

When Buehrig returned to the Auburn-Cord-Duesenberg (A-C-D) group, it was first to restyle Auburns and then to turn his concept for a 'baby Duesy' into the prize-winning 1936–37 Cords, the first cars to have no radiator grille or even an approximation of one. When A-C-D failed he worked for the Budd body company, for Raymond Loewy on Studebakers and then, from 1949 to 1965, at Ford, where he worked on the Continental Mk II. Buehrig continued to create car designs in retirement, patenting the T-top concept sold to General Motors and used on Corvettes for many years.

Harley J. Earl
Vice President, General Motors
American

The most important car stylist of all time, Harley J. Earl was a giant both literally and figuratively. As head of design at General Motors from 1927 – when he began by copying a Hispano-Suiza body design for a 'baby' Cadillac under the La Salle nameplate – until his retirement in 1958, he was autocratically responsible for more than 60 million cars. During his reign GM became the largest, richest and most powerful car manufacturer in the world.

Earl made a few mistakes, including the 'pregnant' 1929 Buick and the three-rear-light 1957 B-body Oldsmobiles and Buicks, but he managed to keep GM the leader in car design throughout most of his long, commercially successful career. And he turned out quite a few cars that most commentators consider absolute masterpieces. His 1938 Y-Job and 1951 Le Sabre one-off prototype cars were shown to the public as dream cars, but Earl drove them to work every day.

Battista 'Pinin' Farina
founder, Carrozzeria Pininfarina
Italian

Starting his career in his brother Giovanni's Stabilimenti Farina in 1904, aged eleven, then going out on his own in 1930 with a magnificent sixteen-cylinder Cadillac, Battista Farina created some of Italy's most beautiful and most intelligent designs. He employed dozens of designers, but no car left his premises until he had approved it himself. He was a pioneer in the activity that saved Italian coachbuilders from extinction: building cars in series for major manufacturers.

There are no British, American or French coachbuilders today, and only Karmann remains in Germany, but Italy has retained three major houses, all following Carrozzeria Pininfarina's business pattern. Farina made a deal with Enzo Ferrari early on, and almost all Ferrari road cars, and many racers as well, have been Pininfarina designs. In 1961 the Italian government granted the descendants of Farina the right to use his nickname and family name combined as their own. Classical beauty is the firm's hallmark.

Joseph Figoni
founder-designer, Figoni
et Falaschi *Italian-French*

Born in Italy at the end of the nineteenth century, Joseph Figoni was a brilliant designer who worked in Plastelene models, not in two-dimensional drawings. He started with a repair shop in 1923, slowly building his business and

his reputation, but by 1933 he was out of both money and possibilities. At that point Ovidio Falaschi, an Italian-born accountant who had married into money, became Figoni's partner and business manager, freeing Figoni to concentrate on design. Having come to France at the age of three, Figoni thought of himself as French, but the French motor industry insisted on thinking of him as a foreigner. Antony Lago, another Italian-born Frenchman, had no qualms about letting Figoni's imagination roam free, and the resulting teardrop-shaped Talbot-Lago Figoni-Falaschi coupés have come to epitomize all that was best in French design during the 1930s. Much prized by collectors today, these wind-tunnel-validated cars stand as Figoni's memorial.

Giorgietto Giugiaro
Italian

Hired very young by Italy's greatest design talent scout, Nuccio Bertone, at the end of the 1950s, Giorgietto Giugiaro quickly blossomed into one of the greatest of all Italian stylists. Always impatient, he moved from Fiat to Bertone, from Bertone to Ghia, and then set up ItalDesign with his friend and partner Aldo Mantovani.

Giugiaro has worked for every car company in the world, he says, "except Honda, and I expect I will work for them one day". Perhaps his most influential design was the original Volkswagen Golf, much imitated

but never surpassed. But his brilliant sports cars, among them several Maseratis and Alfa Romeos and at least one Ferrari, more easily catch the public eye. At any given moment during the past two decades, at least ten Giugiaro designs have been in production all over the world by companies as big as Toyota and VW, and as small as DeLorean and Iso. A true maestro.

Albrecht, Graf Goertz
German-American

Count Goertz, a German nobleman whose mother was Jewish, managed to escape Germany in the late 1930s. In America he discovered and embraced a society completely different from the one he had known in Europe. Applying his manual skills, he ran a hot-rod shop on Rodeo Drive in Beverly Hills decades before this became an upmarket shopping venue.

After joining the US Army he served in the Pacific, and on his discharge as an American citizen he drove the customized Mercury he had built before the war to New York. A chance meeting with Raymond Loewy led to a career in design, despite Loewy's firing him and advising him that he should "marry a rich woman, as you have no talent". Goertz ran a one-man multinational product-design operation from Manhattan for many years, along the way designing two seminal sports cars: the BMW 507 roadster of 1955 and the Datsun 240Z in the early 1970s, both vitally important.

Eugene 'Bob' Gregorie
American

The first official in-house designer for the Ford Motor Company, Bob Gregorie took up the post in the mid-1930s at the request, and with the support, of Edsel Ford, Henry's only son. His first work for the company was shaping the 1932 Ford Y for the company's British arm. Edsel Ford liked this car so much he had the design adapted to the American Ford cars in 1933, and he began a relationship with Gregorie based on mutual admiration and a dedication to elegant vehicles.

Gregorie designed a number of personal cars for Edsel Ford, among them the 1939 Lincoln Continental, later put into production. He innovated in many ways, including putting headlights into the wings of the 1937 Fords and introducing the first application of a horizontally positioned radiator, which created a completely different frontal aspect for cars. Gregorie left Ford in 1946 and never designed another car before he died in 2002.

Jean-Henri Labourdette
French

A third-generation *carrossier*, Jean-Henri Labourdette took over the coachbuilding firm bearing his name when his father died in 1910. With a great deal of flair, and apparently enough business acumen to assure the longevity of his enterprise, he made a brilliant start with his 1912 Turcat-Méry, built for Count Mordvinoff of

Russia. With a pointed tail and mudguards that 'flew' above the rear wheels, this car was of uncommon elegance and embodied his idea of a single curve for the side of the body, from radiator to tail.

In 1913–14 Labourdette designed and built a wooden 'skiff' body on a Panhard chassis for the Chevalier René de Knyff, who suggested the boat-building technique. It was an extraordinary beauty, and led to the construction of many more such boat-shaped cars, consolidating Labourdette's reputation for high style and exceptionally fine quality construction. Later he produced the magnificent history *Un siècle de carrosserie française*, published in 1972.

Anatole Carl Lapine
Latvia, Germany, US

Anatole ('Tony') Lapine followed a long and twisting road from his birthplace in Riga to his position as head of styling for Porsche AG. At the end of the 1930s his family moved from Latvia to Germany because it was 'safer', then to Lincoln, Nebraska, after the war. He joined General Motors Styling as a junior draughtsman while attending engineering courses at night. He moved from the huge drafting room to a 'toy shop' studio with just one stylist for company.

When that studio shut down, Lapine returned to Germany, working in GM's Adam Opel studios. It was there that he met Dr Ferdinand 'Ferry' Porsche, who invited him to head Porsche

Design when the company was purged of Porsche family members in operating roles. Until Lapine retired, with the exception of the 911 and 914, all Porsche production-car projects (924, 928, 959) were created under his direction.

Patrick Le Quément
British-French

Born to a French father and a British mother, Patrick Le Quément was sent to a boarding school in England at the age of eleven when his father died, and thus grew up bicultural and bilingual despite possessing a French passport and fierce loyalty to France. His design studies at the Birmingham Institute of Art prepared him for a career in car design, which he began at Simca.

After a period as an independent product designer, Le Quément found a place with Ford in Britain. The company then moved him to Germany, Brazil, Australia, Japan and the USA. He did not like the Ford operation at Dearborn, so he joined Volkswagen, setting up an advanced design centre in Düsseldorf. He was invited to Renault by its enlightened chief executive Raymond Lévy, and given free rein to do whatever he thought necessary to make Renault a design leader. That he has done so brilliantly is demonstrated by his numerous design awards and the company's commercial success.

Sir William Lyons
British

Britain's finest-ever stylist was first and foremost a tough, capable businessman. But he possessed an innate sense of line and form and an unbeatable sense of what would sell if made available at accessible prices. His cars were rarely completely original, but whatever his inspiration he typically vastly improved what he borrowed – as shown by his transformation of a podgy pre-war BMW 328 by Touring into the iconic Jaguar XK120, or his gorgeous 'Cad's Bentley' saloons of the 1930s.

Sir William neither drew nor modelled. Working outdoors with a favourite panel beater, he directed the shaping of actual sheet metal into the first example of each of his designs. He was a noted penny-pincher, and Jaguar quality always suffered from his corner cutting, earning a reputation for unreliability that only the cars' sheer beauty counterbalanced. Every Jaguar today owes its appearance to work done by Sir William before he retired in 1972.

Giovanni Michelotti
Italian

The most prolific of all Italian car designers, Michelotti provided imaginative and practical sketches of new designs to anyone who asked, whether a corner body shop in Turin or a prime coach-builder, putting his stamp on

literally thousands of one-off Fiat-based cars. Often he asked for only a pittance, and more often than not managed to collect not even that. At one Turin Motor Show in the early 1950s he had more than fifty cars on exhibition.

Michelotti's designs for Ferraris for Alfredo Vignale, who got his start making bodies for Cisitalia cars, were among the most beautiful of all time, with a purity of line and detail that belied their intended purpose: to be pure racing cars. Fortunately for his finances, Michelotti also shaped cars for Triumph in Britain, BMW in Germany, Alpine in France and for other major manufacturers.

Amos E. Northrup
American

In his forty-eight years Amos E. Northrup had a tremendous influence on American car design. He began his career as a furniture designer, moved to trucks with Pierce-Arrow, switched to the Murray Corporation (body builder to many manufacturers), then to Willys and back to Murray, where he created striking bodies for Hudson, Hupmobile, Reo, Ford and Willys, as well as his last radical design, the 1938 Graham. He found time along the way to create an ocean liner and a streamlined railway locomotive.

Northrup's striking 1932 Graham Blue Streak introduced the idea of monochromatic paint schemes – radical in an era when striping and contrasting colours

of articulated elements of body and bumpers were common. In the 1980s the idea arose again with German specialists such as AMG, but Northrup the innovator was there long before. His greatest contribution to design was in integrating disparate elements into a coherent whole, as he did with the 1931 Reo Royale and then the 1938 Graham.

Ferruccio Palamidessi
Italian

Quiet, unassuming Ferruccio Palamidessi was a bodywork designer at Alfa Romeo in Milan. In the early post-war years 'Pal' created the first sketches and layouts of the Giulietta Sprint coupé later built by Bertone, after minor retouching by Nuccio Bertone, Franco Scaglione, Mario Boano and Tiberio Gracco de Lay. The original drawing, exhibited at the Turin Motor Show in 1992, is unequivocal: Pal designed the Sprint.

At that time the designer had never before ridden in a car. His one ride before leaving for America in 1955, when Harley Earl hired him for General Motors, was through the streets of Milan at insane speeds in a 1930s Alfa 2900 roadster, then one of the fastest cars in the world, driven by factory racer Clemente Biondetti. Earl never understood the little man who was one of the few who had the courage to contradict him, but the two had a relationship of mutual respect that produced excellent results.

Bruno Sacco
Italian-German

Italian-born German citizen Bruno Sacco began his design career in the 1950s at Carrozzeria Ghia with Giovanni Savonuzzi, but dreamed of working in Germany because as a child he had been so deeply impressed by Märklin toy trains, made with astonishing precision. So when he presented some of his work to Daimler-Benz and was offered a post with the venerable firm, he seized the opportunity. Working in the body-engineering department before moving to styling gave him an edge in this engineering-oriented company.

Honoured professionally as 'the designer's designer', Sacco led Mercedes from traditional upright designs into the modern era of aerodynamics. His 190-Class 'baby Mercedes' of 1982 presaged more modern and efficient Mercedes styling, and led to such innovations as a Mercedes station wagon, the mono-volume A-Class and even the Smart city car, truly a radical innovation for Daimler-Benz. All the while he preserved the character and quality of the marque.

Franco Scaglione
Italian

Little known today, aeronautical engineer Franco Scaglione was one of many designers 'discovered' and nurtured by Giuseppe 'Nuccio' Bertone, very possibly the greatest of them. In the early 1950s Scaglione created the astonishing Bertone Aerodinamico Tecnico studies, BATs 5, 7 and 9. With their extreme tail fins, rounded windscreens and extremely low drag coefficients, they were beyond style. His Alfa Romeo Sportiva, a four-cylinder 2-litre car, was so cleverly shaped that its top speed was greater than that of the Mercedes 300 SL of the same period.

Not the easiest of men to work with, Scaglione stayed in Bertone's good graces for eight years (1952–60), during which time he created some forty designs, all beautifully surfaced and good to look at, whether stylistically restrained, as in the 1954 Aston Martin DB4 cabriolet, or extreme, as in the BAT series. He also created the first Lamborghinis for Carrozzeria Touring and a few one-off cars before virtually disappearing from car design.

John Tjaarda and Tom Tjaarda
Dutch-American

Father-and-son car designers are not particularly unusual. Even so, in the case of the Tjaardas one is struck by their first-rank contributions to car design over such a long period. John, born in The Netherlands in 1897, went to America in 1923 and began work at the Locke body company. Trained in aerodynamics, adept in structures and a fine stylist, he created his most significant car in 1936, the Lincoln Zephyr. As big a success as an aerodynamic design as the Chrysler Airflow was a failure, the Zephyr saved Lincoln from oblivion. Although John's

unit-construction engineering was used, Henry Ford insisted on keeping his Model T-style suspension rather than the all-independent system Tjaarda created.

His son, Stevens Thompson ('Tom') Tjaarda van Sterkenberg, was born in 1934. He trained as an architect at the University of Michigan but after graduating went to Italy to work at Ghia. He subsequently worked on the Turin Millennium exposition under the presidency of Battista 'Pinin' Farina, after which he joined Carrozzeria Pininfarina as a designer. He designed two Ferraris, including the legendary 'California Spyder' and the Fiat 124 roadster.

After a period as chief designer at Ghia, where he created the original Ford Fiesta and designed the De Tomaso Pantera, and another as director of advanced design at Fiat, Tom established his own consultancy in Turin. He has designed more than fifty cars, and continues to work for the world's leading car manufacturers. The latest Honda Civic employs his input, more than eighty years after his father's first efforts in car design.

GLOSSARY OF MOTORING TERMS AND STYLES

N.B.: This is a glossary of UK terms, with American terms expressed in square brackets where appropriate.

A-pillar, B-pillar, C-pillar, D-pillar
Vertical roof-support posts that form part of a car's bodywork. The A-pillar sits at the outer ends of the windscreen [windshield] on closed bodies. By extension, the pillars at the rear of the front doors (*i.e.* between the front and rear doors) on are B-pillars, those between the rear doors and rear or rear-side windows are C-pillars, and on some estate cars [station wagons] and limousines there are D-pillars as well.

Alloy wheels
Refers generally to lighter-than-steel metals, *i.e.* aluminium or magnesium alloys. Early examples were seen on Bugatti racing cars from 1924 and on Bugatti road cars from 1926. Today, all high performance cars use them, and most ordinary cars have cast alloy wheels available at least as optional equipment.

Artillery wheel
Typically a wooden-spoke wheel with steel rim to which the tyre was mounted. Used until late 1930s and now obsolete.

Backlight
Rearmost transverse window or windows in a car body, opposed to windscreen [windshield].

Beltline (or waistline)
The area of the body just below the side window-glass and the various pillars in the roof.

Bezel
Trim piece, usually of bright material, separating one element on a body from another; for example the ring securing the glass of a headlamp to the surrounding body parts. Also used inside the car to describe the surrounds of instruments and switches on the **dashboard**.

Boat-tail
Rear bodywork resembling the inverted prow of a small boat. Usually, but not always, applied to open cars, especially **roadsters**.

Bonnet [hood]
The bodywork panel or panels covering the engine compartment of a vehicle.

Bumper
A protective bar or form, normally horizontal. at the front and rear of a body; in modern cars often encapsulated within a plastic **fascia**.

Casting
A process in which a liquid is poured into or over a form to capture its surface. Where the liquid is molten metal, casting is used to manufacture raw parts for mechanical and body elements. Wet plaster is often used for making a mould into which another material can be poured in order to make a functional part. Also, the part so formed.

Catwalk
The panel between front **wing** [fender] and **bonnet** [hood] on cars, typically used between 1930 and 1950.

Chassis
The underlying structural basis of automobiles from the early days, comprising an open framework to which all mechanical elements were attached and on to which bodies could be placed. Vincenzo Lancia began the integration of body and chassis as a single structural unit at the beginning of the 1920s, and most modern cars use the body for structural strength, eliminating the heavy frame.

Coachbuilder
A specialist in car body construction. especially in the three decades between 1920 and 1950. Mass production has virtually eliminated such enterprises, but firms such as Pininfarina in Italy, Karmann in Germany and Heuliez in France make a living by producing niche models in small series, for example Volkswagen and Peugeot coupés and convertibles.

Concept
The idea from which a car design begins. A concept sketch can lead to, and through, the entire process of creating a concept car, the purpose of which is to offer new ideas for consideration.

Concours d'Elégance — Literally, an elegance contest. First used in France in the 1920s as a competition between stylish society women, who used coachbuilders and couturiers to enhance their standing. A car would be driven on stage and a fashionably dressed woman would emerge, make a tour around the car (perhaps accompanied by a dog), re-enter the car and drive off. The practice was revived briefly in Italy after World War II and was subsequently adopted by American car collectors as a static show of cars only. The doyen of modern Concours has been held at Pebble Beach, California, since 1950, but the character of all modern events was established in 1955, when racing driver Phil Hill, later Formula One World Champion, presented his self-restored 1931 Pierce-Arrow. Since then, a post-World War II car has taken Best in Show, the most coveted prize in all Concours, only once.

Dash
A panel ahead of the seat on horse-drawn vehicles, carried over to some horseless carriages such as the Curved Dash Oldsmobile.

Dashboard
As engines moved forward of the passenger compartment, the wall separating them became known as the dashboard. By extension, the term was applied to the instrument panel once this had moved back from the **firewall**.

Deck
The upper surface of rear luggage compartment on modern envelope body cars, usually horizontal.

Disc wheel
A wheel in which the central portion (spider) is made of pressed sheet metal and welded, riveted or bolted to the rim.

Dogleg
A kinked section in a line of bodywork.

Drip moulding Also known as the rain gutter, a small applied section above the side doors intended to keep water gathered on the roof from falling on to passengers entering or exiting a car.

Drivetrain
The vehicle propulsion system apart from the engine, including clutch, transmission, propeller shaft and axle.

Envelope body
A full-width body that covers both wheels and passenger sections with no protuberances; a **pontoon body**.

Facelift
A term used to describe the refreshing of body shapes and details.

Fascia
A cover for the structural parts of a front or rear bumper; the panel containing the instruments, switches and minor controls located in front of the driver; see **dashboard**.

Fastback
Term used to describe bodywork in which the roof profile continues in a single convex curve from windscreen header to the rear extremity of the body.

Firewall
A metal panel separating the engine compartment from the passenger space.

Flange
A section of material typically turned at right angles to the larger surface of which it is part. Flanges are used to join thin materials,

usually by spot welding, but also with adhesives or mechanical fasteners such as bolts or rivets.

Greenhouse
The car's upper body; the glazed area of the passenger compartment that sits above the car's waistline (beltline).

Grille
At first a purely functional addition to a radiator assembly, a wire-mesh grille was placed in front of the fragile radiator core to protect it from stones thrown up by other cars. Later, when it had been integrated with the **radiator shell**, it was made into a decorative element for marque identity.

Hardtop
A roof for a convertible that can be removed; also, by misconception (as used in the American term 'hardtop convertible'), a body style in which the side glass could descend entirely, as in a convertible, but with a fixed steel roof panel that remained in place. In the 1950s there were 'four-door hardtops', which retained a B-pillar only below the waistline (beltline) of the body. Expensive to manufacture, the style disappeared with the generalization of air conditioning.

Hood [top]
A fabric structure of defined form that covers the passenger compartment of a car, able to be folded to allow passengers to ride exposed to the elements. Now also used to describe a hard roof capable of being removed entirely or folded into the luggage compartment.

Hood cover [top boot]
A fabric panel or hard material covering the folded fabric of a convertible top to protect it from sun, wind and rain.

Independent suspension
Most early vehicles had wheels attached to each end of an axle running across the entire width of the car. A bump encountered by one wheel would therefore upset the other wheel on the same axle. Although there were pioneers who saw the necessity of isolating each wheel with its own springing (e.g. Morgan, Lancia), front axles persisted until the 1950s (Datsun), and rear axles are still in common use in America, for cars as well as for light trucks. Independent suspension, in which all wheels can rise and fall separately of each other, improves ride comfort, handling and safety.

Instrument panel
The section of the interior that presents vital operating information to the driver. Ultimately the only data really required are speed and quantity of fuel remaining.

Light
A car window, other than the windscreen [windshield]. Americans use the term 'backlight' for the rear window, but speak of a 'three-window coupé'. British practice is to define body styles using side lights only, thus 'four-light saloon', discounting the rear transverse window.

Louvre [louver]
An indentation or protuberance on a thin panel, usually appearing in tightly spaced rows, that allows

hot air to exit an engine compartment.

Magneto
Essentially a primitive spark generator. It uses an engine-driven rotating shaft that cuts lines of magnetic force in order to create high-voltage electrical charges that can be sent to spark plugs. Magnetos are still used on light aircraft piston engines, the principal virtue of a magneto being that it is not dependent on any external source for an electric current. Its principal fault is that the timing of the spark cannot easily be altered as the engine speed varies. This is not a problem in aircraft engines, which typically run at a constant speed, but is not compatible with modern microchip-controlled integrated fuel-injection systems.

Moulding [molding]
A raised section, either incorporated in a body panel pressing or applied to a simple panel for decoration.

Monocoque
Properly used of car bodies to describe a structure wherein all panels are of the same thickness. The first series-produced monocoque car was the Saab 92, the second the early 1950s Austin A30 Seven. Designing a true monocoque requires great skill, but the term is often applied to **unitized** bodies with a mixture of thick and thin members.

NACA duct
A geometric shape positioned beneath the normal surface of an aerodynamic form in order to take in passing air with the minimum

of resistance. Developed by the National Advisory Committee on Aeronautics (now NASA), the duct was used first on jet aeroplanes before being adapted for racing cars.

Notchback
A car in which there is a distinct separation of roof and rear **deck** at the base of the rear window.

One-off
A design made with no intention of eventual replication, thus not a **prototype**.

Overhang
The distance from the centre of the front wheel (i.e. the axle) to the vehicle's foremost extremity, or from the centre of the rear wheel to the rearmost extremity. Front overhang, plus wheelbase, plus rear overhang equals overall length.

Package
Term referring to the way in which disparate elements are placed in a car: mechanics, passenger space, luggage space, fuel storage etc.

Phaeton
An alternative word for **tourer**, more commonly used in America.

Planetary gearbox
Planetary gear sets consist of a central sun gear mounted on a shaft, in mesh with a series of planetary gears surrounding it; they in turn are meshed with a surrounding ring gear with internal teeth. The ratio of input to output speed depends on which gears are kept locked in place, usually by friction bands. Because the gears are constantly in mesh, there are

no problems of sliding teeth into engagement. The Model T Ford had a two-speed planetary gearbox and was relatively easy to drive compared to its contemporaries. Typical modern automatic gearboxes use several planetary gear sets in series to obtain multiple ratios, giving anywhere between three and seven forward speeds or ratios.

Platform
A term that replaces the classic 'chassis' for **unitized** construction. In recent years it has been defined as a set of common points. Some cars have 'corners' (*i.e.* suspension units) that can be spaced laterally and longitudinally to give different **packages** that still use identical elements. Individual models can vary in size and shape yet still be considered to use a common platform. In this way some major manufacturers obtain as many as a dozen models from the same platform.

Pontoon or **pontoon body**
This term refers to full-width bodywork with through **wings**.

Prototype
The initial model of a car. In early practice, the first car made to a new design might well have been sold to a customer, but today it is legally forbidden to sell any vehicle that has not been certified to meet standards – a process that requires the destructive testing of prototypes.

Quarter panel
The exterior body panel behind the side door, below the waistline (beltline) and directly above the rear **wing**.

Quarter light [quarter window]
A triangular-shaped window fitted to the forward edge of a front door.

Radiator
Typically a liquid-to-air heat exchanger, today used on all cars to cool the engine and provide heat for passengers. Air-cooled cars were common until pollution-control considerations made their use impossible, Volkswagen being the last proponent.

Radiator shell
The actual heat-exchanger part of a radiator consists of tubes and thin fins arranged in a honeycomb-like manner, usually with a tank affixed top and bottom. In early cars, there tended to be a skin of bright metal applied around the outside of the working parts, with the whole remaining visible. As the automobile developed, the protective function of grilles was subsumed to one of decoration and marque identity, with each manufacturer seeking a unique, readily recognized look. Good examples include the Parthenon-shaped grille of Rolls-Royce, and the horseshoe-shaped radiator and grille assemblies of Bugattis.

Roadster
An open two-seater passenger car.

Rocker panel
The lower extremity of a unitized body car, normally shaped and painted as part of the body design.

Scoop
A protuberance on the exterior of a vehicle's surface, the purpose of which is to take in air for the purposes of cooling or ventilation. It was often used on racing cars, especially in the 1950s, before greater aerodynamic knowledge led to lower drag negative inlets such as the **NACA duct**.

Scuttle [cowl]
The part of a car's bodywork between the rearmost edge of the **bonnet** and the leading edge of the front doors. Typically this section included the **firewall** and was produced by the chassis manufacturer and passed on to the coachbuilder. The best coach-builders, nonetheless, chose to build the **scuttle**, **bonnet** and **wings**, even if they were supplied with a base chassis incorporating those elements.

Section
Term applied to a transverse cut through the body of a car, perpendicular to its centreline plane. (The section of a cylinder is a circle.)

Sill
The lower extremity of a car body.

Tourer
An open car with a minimum of four seats and a folding hood.

Track [tread]
The distance between the centre of a tyre and its opposite on the same axle. For many years almost all cars had the same dimension, identical to that of Roman chariots, early railroads etc. Before there were paved roads, it was important that all vehicles, animal-drawn or powered, should be able to run in the same ruts.

Tumblehome
A term derived from marine practice that defines the inward slope of side windows from their base towards the roof.

Tyre [tire]
A flexible tension envelope, typically made from woven fibres of synthetic resins (rayon, nylon) and/or steel wire covered with natural or synthetic rubber.

Unitized (or unit) body
Now virtually standard for cars, and becoming so for light trucks used as personal transport, unit bodies incorporate the structural functions of separate chassis with the bodywork, thereby assuring a vehicle at once lighter and stronger than can be achieved by separated units.

Valance
A sheet of sometimes preformed metal to enhance the lines of a car or to obscure unsightly body parts.

Wheel cover
A metal panel often used to hide wire wheels on early cars, often now a plastic moulding that covers a steel disk wheel. Curiously, these almost always simulate a cast light-alloy wheel.

Wheelhouse
The volume of space within the bodywork devoted to an individual wheel. As a wheel moves upwards over a bump in the road, turns to accomplish steering, or does both at once, it describes a volume that must be kept free of any element that might touch a wheel, tyre or snow chain that might be attached. By extension, the term is commonly used to designate the actual opening in the body skin through which the wheel and tyre can be seen.

Wing [fender]
The original bicycle term was 'mudguard', and the function has always been the same: to keep mud, water, snow, slush and other unpleasant materials away from the driver and passenger. To be totally effective, there needs to be a connection between the wings and the body, and eventually the disparate elements of a car have tended to fuse into a single simple shape encompassing all contents.

Wing spat [fender skirt]
A panel that covers the rear wheel (exceptionally a front wheel on certain French cars of the 1930s), integrating into the rear wing opening.

Wire wheel
There are two kinds of wire wheels: the classic tension-spoke wheel invented by Sir George Cayley, and the later welded compression-spoke type used by Henry Ford in the 1920s and 1930s. In the first, the hub actually hangs from the upper spokes; in the second, it reposes upon the column represented by several wires. In the early days of the car, wire wheels were considerably lighter than wooden-spoke wheels and so were preferred for sporting models. Wire wheels do not resist side loads well, and are considerably heavier than cast, forged or even pressed-steel disk, wheels. They are lovely to look at, diabolical to keep clean, and exist today purely as decoration.

DIRECTORY OF MUSEUMS AND COLLECTIONS

Surprisingly, there are literally thousands of automotive museums around the world (Google lists 33,800), ranging from small collections, such as Formula One world champion Michael Schumacher's personal racing cars, on display at his family's kart track in Germany, to the Autostadt ('Car City') in Volkswagen's home town of Wolfsburg. This complex contains individual museums for each of the group's six storied marques: VW, Audi, Bentley, Bugatti, Lamborghini, Seat and Skoda.

Car manufacturers often maintain one-make museums of their own models, among which the Mercedes-Benz and Porsche collections in Stuttgart are especially significant. Some producers take a wider view: Toyota, for example, has a splendid museum housing a variety of other makers' cars. The Henry Ford Museum in Dearborn, Michigan, was started by the Ford Motor Company when Henry owned it outright, but is now fully independent. It is, in effect, a museum of technology, in which one can follow the development of ordinary machines, from household refrigerators to farm tractors and aircraft. It is set in a park-like environment, Greenfield Village, to which the actual laboratory in which Thomas Edison developed the electric lamp, and the Wright brothers' house from Dayton, Ohio, have been transported and resurrected. The Deutsches Museum in Munich is close to it in spirit, with much more than cars on view and each object placed in its proper cultural context.

Following is a selection of some of the best car museums around the world.

Argentina
Fundación Museo del Automovilismo "Juan Manuel Fangio"
Mitre, Balcarce, R.A. 7620
Tel. +54 (0)266 25540

Australia
National Motor Museum
Shannon Street
Birdwood, Adelaide
South Australia 5234
Tel. +61 08 8568 5006

France
Musée National de l'Automobile de Mulhouse
Collection Schlumpf
192 avenue de Colmar
BP 1096
68051 Mulhouse cedex
Tel. +33 (0)3 89 33 23 33

Germany
Deutsches Museum
Museumsinsel 1
D-80538 Munich
Tel. +49 (0)89 2179 1

Mercedes-Benz Museum
Mercedesstrasse 137/1
73027 Stuttgart
Tel. +49 (0)711 172 578

Technik-Museum Speyer
Geibstrasse 2
D-67436 Speyer
Tel. +49 (0)6232 6708 0

Italy
Galleria Ferrari
Via Dino Ferrari 43
41053 Maranello (MO)
Tel. +39 0536 943204

Museo dell'Automobile
Carlo Biscaretti di Ruffia
Corso Unità d'Italia 40
10126 Torino
Tel. +39 011 677 666/7/8

Japan
Motor Car Museum of Japan
40 Ikkanyama, Futatsunashi-cho
Komatsu, Ishhikawa
J-923-0345
Tel. +81 (0)761 43 4343

Toyota Automobile Museum
Nagakute-cho, Aichi-ken
J-480-11
Tel. +81 (0)561 63 5151

The Netherlands
National Automobile Museum
(Nationaal Automobielmuseum)
Steurweg 8
4941 VR Raamsdonksveer
(Noord-Brabant)
Tel. +31 (0) 162 585400

Russia
Polytechnical Museum
Novaya ploschad 3/4
101000 Moscow
Tel. +7 (095) 921 52 94

Sweden
Museum of Technology
(Sveriges Tekniska Museet)
Museivägen 7
115 93 Stockholm
Tel. +46 (0) 8 450 5600

Switzerland
Musée International de l'Automobile
Voie-des-Trax 40
Hall 7, Palexpo
CH-1218 Grand Saconnex
Geneva
Tel. +41 (0)22.788.84.84

United Kingdom
National Motor Museum
Beaulieu
Brockenhurst
Hampshire SO42 7ZN
Tel. +44 (0)1590 612345

USA
Harrah National Automobile Museum
10 Lake Street South
Reno, NV 89501
Tel. +1 702 333 9300

Henry Ford Museum and Greenfield Village
20900 Oakwood Boulevard
Dearborn, MI 48124-2455
Tel. +1 313 982 6150

Imperial Palace Auto Collection
Imperial Palace Hotel and Casino
3535 Las Vegas Boulevard South
Las Vegas, NV 89109
Tel. +1 702 794 3174

Indianapolis Motor Speedway Hall of Fame Museum
4790 West 16th Street
Indianapolis, IN 46222
Tel. +1 317 181 8500

The Petersen Automotive Museum
6060 Wilshire Boulevard
Los Angeles, CA 90036
Tel. +1 323 930 2277

INDEX